Edit

Crazy For Creatures

A Collection Of Animal Poetry

First published in Great Britain in 2009 by:

forward**press**

Forward Press
Remus House
Coltsfoot Drive
Peterborough
PE2 9JX
Telephone: 01733 890099
Website: www.forwardpress.co.uk

Foreword

Everyone at Forward Press would like to
thank all the authors and contributors in this
collection, for their truly wild and wonderful
entries. It is always a great pleasure to receive
and read through the many celebrations of
friendship and happiness that you share with
all creatures great and small.

Wriggling, pouncing and leaping onto the
pages of this book are the anecdotes and
tales of hundreds of much-loved furry friends,
creepy critters and beautiful beasts. Delve
inside to read authors' poetry of admiration
and adoration towards their own pets, and
take a look at some of the contributors'
favourite animal snaps.

Loyalty, companionship, and a love for nature,
help make 'Crazy For Creatures' exactly what
it is: warming, funny and sometimes a little bit
curious! Now, dive in and enjoy some of our
favourite poems showing the wonders of the
animal kingdom.

Contents

Lipson Community College, Plymouth

The Poems

The Many Names Of Rabetoefix

We have a rabbit, which has had many, many names,
And when we let him into the garden, he played many games,
His first name was Rabetoefix, to sound like a name of Gaul,
And once it was just, an ordinary name like Paul.

At the top of the garden he had a large run,
But whenever he was fed, carrots he would shun.
He would push the footballs around with his nose
And would often jump up, meeting the sky with his toes.

One day, my brother called the rabbit Harry
And then, a week later, changed its name to Gary.
On another day, he started to call it Fred
And many more names after the ones that I have just said.

In the far left corner, he'd dig up the soil
The more he digs, the more it will spoil.
He'd run, he'd hop, he'd jump, he'd dance,
Then run to the corner and try to dig to France!

Once again, he gained a new name
But like all the others, the duration was the same.
He'd have it a week, maybe less, maybe more,
And he'd have a different name again by the time he'd passed the door.

Once we found a frog, inside his large run
It must have been living there a while to shelter from the sun.
The rabbit didn't acknowledge the frog, they never did fight
And the frog would always stay inside the run, in the darkness of night.

Our rabbit's been called, John, George, Ringo and Paul
Harry, Fred and Rabetoefix, from Gaul.
I haven't mentioned all his names here
The full list would surely take about a year.
He's had many names, he's played many games
Maybe with luck, he'll keep the name James.

James Harper

Ruby At Home

I'm new to the family
Ruby's the name
And everything's lovely
I'm so glad I came.

There's a rabbit called Bobby
And a lurcher named Ted,
And everyone's lovely. I think I've just said
A garden to play in, on long walks I go
I'm over the moon, have I told you so?

I belong to the family
I'm everyone's pet
I'm so happy to be here my tail's wagging yet.
But . . . Sarah's my best friend
Cos right from the start
This sweet little girl has stolen my heart.

Best friends forever, I know we will be
Oh, I'm so glad to be here with my new family.

Jacqueline Claire Davies

Lapin Rabbit

Lapin rabbit was his name
Chasing bunnies was his game
Met a doe named Daisy-Sue
Loved the colour of her eyes' hue
Taught her everything he knew
Was not long before she shared his name
Big ones, little ones, all alike
Jumping around in great delight
Now old Lapin rabbit dreams of the past
Because today he's only half-fast.

Victorine Lejeune-Stubbs

Dog Is Too Small A Word

You're there when I wake up, there when I sleep,
A head on my lap, a paw on my knee.
When life lets me down, you help me carry on.
Dog is too small a word.

Best friend, comforter in grief,
A soulmate to talk to, walk with and love.
Brown eyes so deep and so true, your mouth never lies.
Dog is too small a word.

Never demanding, never cross,
Forever contented and full of fun.
You take joy in the simple things, a run on the beach.
Dog is too small a word.

There with a cuddle, a nose on my hand,
You keep me going when life gets me down.
Always there, always true, your love stays solid whatever I do.
Dog is too small a word.

Linda Lewis

My Dog

My dog's name is Bo,
She's just a little monkey!
She always rolls in poo
And smells a bit funky.

My dog's name is Bo,
She even answers back!
She clacks her teeth together
But, of course, she never gets a smack.

My dog's name is Bo,
She chewed my favourite shorts,
And I still don't forgive her
But I love her despite her faults.

My dog's name is Bo,
Mum rescued her,
But I'm glad she did,
She's like (in French) my soeur!

Danielle Frensham

Pippin

My cat.
My friend.
A psychic bond.
Together we
For so very long.

Pain for him
Was pain for me
Decision hard
To set him free.

So from my arms
His spirit flew
To find sweet peace
In places new.

In love he met
His final end.
I shed my tears
For my cat,
My friend.

Miki Byrne

King Of The Cul-De-Sac

Rommel was a bruiser - there is no other word;
He terrorised the neighbourhood; each night he could be heard
Yowling like a banshee from at least a mile away.
You never saw him sleeping - not even through the day.

The streets would be patrolled religiously each hour;
He rarely stopped to groom or take shelter from a shower.
To say he was quite raucous would be an understatement;
He soon became notorious with the local Noise Abatement.

His ears were all in tatters, his nose a mass of sores;
Due to his pugnacious nature he was always in the wars.
The whiskers, though once plentiful, had rapidly diminished;
His fighting days, had he not died, were truly far from finished.

A previous encounter with the tom from Orchard Crescent
Had rendered his whole countenance remarkably unpleasant.
His owners were beside themselves - the vet fees cost a packet -
Quite unaware that Rommel ran his own protection racket.

But this battle-scarred old moggy met a most untimely end:
It was in the early hours when a truck sped round the bend.
Poor Rommel didn't stand a chance - he'd finally met his match;
The time had come to relinquish his long-defended patch.

I wonder where he is right now, our war-worn feline friend;
Despite his former health and strength, his life now at an end.
Will he be resting peacefully amid angelic glow,
Or will he be consorting with the devil down below?

Heather Pickering

Chichi

My precious Chichi
Is no longer here
He was black
And his coat was
Groomed with care
And the children loved him
For he was funny as well
He would steal
Their backpacks
And hide them for them to find
'Chichi, you have won the game
I want to get off to school'
From behind the sofa
He would fish his find
With a grin
That was as splendid as air.

Carolle Cole Pemberton

Man's Best Friend

With a wag of his tail he likes to greet you,
He tries to comfort you when you're feeling blue;
Your secrets he won't ever tell,
When you're not dressed up, he loves you just as well;
He seems to listen to your every word
And walkies is the best sound he's ever heard;
His idea of Heaven is a game in the park
And curling up beside the fire when it grows dark;
All he craves is some of your attention,
Treat him kindly and he'll return your affection;
Though his feelings for you are unspoken,
His loyalty and devotion will never be broken.

Annabelle Tipper

Our Goldfish

With glistening scales
And their big boggly eyes,
Their effortless glide where the
Treasure chest lies,
Their attraction never fails.

We look at them,
They look at us,
I wonder what they think?
With their knowing looks
And playful pranks,
Our spirits never sink.

Darting shapes in the calm green gloom,
Nibbling weed and turning stones,
Cleaning out their tank to groans
We'll always have the room!

Tina Knight

Petrified

Staying in a house on the bleak rugged moors
I needed from work to unwind
I slumped in my chair with book in my hand
Large gin and a sandwich I dined.

I started to read when scratching I heard
I felt uneasy, a strange presence amid
Looking up the door opened slowly
Such panic unable to rid.

Petrified I sat upright in my seat
I turned my head, but no one was there
I wanted to shout, but my mouth was dry
With terror I clung to my chair.

My heart was pounding, I thought it would burst
A breeze brushed over my feet
A prickly feeling went up my back
Then pressure, and stabbing and heat.

Feeling something around my neck
Surely it wasn't a ghost
Warm air of breathing close to my ear
The parrot was playing my host.

Catherine M Armstrong

Diplodactylus Damaeus

I do not envy
the gecko's ability
to cleanse its eyeballs

of debris and dust
by wiping them with its broad,
pliant, snake-like tongue -

a manoeuvre I
neither seek to emulate
nor wish to master.

On the other hand,
it might be useful to have
fine coloration,

exquisite markings
and its chameleon gift
of camouflaged skin,

its ability
to become invisible,
blend in, disappear.

Norman Bissett

Lap Dog

I've got a dog,
He sleeps like a log.
He likes to bite feet,
Finds bad things to eat.
He doesn't know a trick,
He doesn't even do lick!
Puts my patience to the test,
But I love him best
When he climbs up on my knee.
Then it's just Storm, my English Setter, and me.

Clare Todd

My Little Friend

He came to join the family
A lively bundle of fur
Who quickly adapted to our home
Winding around our legs with a purr.
The children he taunted with glee
Leaving many a scratch with his claws,
That were difficult to control
Stretching out at the end of his paws.
A slender and sleek gent he grew
With a shiny coat black as jet,
Sedately walking everywhere
So quiet and arrogant in his way, and yet
The racket he transmitted at meal times
Could be heard for many a mile
Making us run for the ear plugs
To blot it all out for a while.
When fed he made for the telly
To watch one of his favourite shows,
With a cat as lovely as Lucky
My heart always had a glow.

Daphne Fryer

The Lodger

When I lifted the lid on the half-barrel
someone had circled into the kitchen
there was the surprise
of the jackdaw,
his pale blue eyes quick and observant,
his charcoal wing splayed
at an odd angle.

The day he balanced on the rim
we knew we'd lost
that little crow
with the grey-silver shawl
admired at close quarters.

He took the kitchen in his stride,
insinuated the hoary shale of his beak
into our palms, insisted on service
in loud metallic tones.

Though we knew him to be
a natural scavenger at heart,
we missed that Jack in the park,
that petty thief who'd snatch
your scrap of silver,
that knave who'd live in your chimney.

Margaret Galvin

On My Own

Don't leave me too long alone all day
When you go to work to earn your pay.
I know you have a job to do
But I miss you.

Don't leave me to watch a fly on the wall
Or to see a clumsy spider crawl
Or to watch leaves drifting as they fall.
I miss you.

Don't leave me,
Again, it's a lovely day,
Can we go for a walk? Can we play?
Are you going to work again today?
I miss you.

Don't go, tell me what have I done wrong
For you to leave me alone so long?
I'm sure you love me,
I know you do!
I miss you.

Do I have to hear the key lock the door?
When it closes behind you like before
I'm alone in the house once more,
I miss you.

I love the chair you gave to me
So through the window I can see.
But I'm alone again
There's only me
I miss you.

It's quiet, so quiet, there's no one home
Nothing moves when I'm on my own.
Are you thinking of me here all alone?
I miss you.

When I'm alone I cannot eat,
I just lay listening to the sounds of your feet
Or the car pulling up outside in the street.
I miss you.

I love you Mum you know it's true
Don't leave me so often, here without you.
What am I supposed to do?
I miss you.

Where's my lead, can I come too?
Am I going out for a walk with you?
Please don't say it's only you,
I miss you.

I'm bored and tired of hours alone
I love you so much, please come home.
I'll be good I promise, I'll leave you alone
Then you'll be here and I . . .
Won't miss you anymore.

Jenny Pederson

The Trouble With Muddle

My budgie called Muddle
Was sat in a puddle
Looking so sad and ill
He does as he pleases
But soon caught the sneezes
Like budgies so often will
He sneezed at the cat
He sneezed at the dog
He sneezed at the telly too
To double my trouble
He popped like a bubble
And left with an atishoo!

Poor Muddle was muddled
And I was in trouble
I had to think what to do
I thought out aloud
Then said I know how
I'll stick him together with glue
The plan worked so well
You just couldn't tell
That budgie was once in two
And then I declared
The name isn't fair
So Muddle's now called UHU.

T Parry

Playful Mouse

I saw a mouse this very day
It didn't quickly run away
As it had come out to play
Its coat so grey, its ears were pricked
It looked at me as if to say
'I'll come out and play with you today.'

Robert Walker

You Soppy Dog Walkers!

I'm sitting, watching on the wall -
while you and your pets tramp by.
Regardless of the weather, canines
need two daily walks, as a rule.
Wearing plush coats, they stay bone-dry
to us cats, that's asinine!

We take ourselves out for a walk,
(though not so much on rainy days.)
Then, there are walls and trees to climb
or field, and house rodents to stalk.
Local councils decide your ways,
and showers turn grassy paths to slime.

Bedraggled mutts, who tried the lake
on for size, are in for a bath
and so are you, walkers, with legs
mud-splattered whenever they shake
themselves, as a bathing aftermath -
spreading, too the lake-bed's dregs.

Cats may well contemplate the sin
of fish-pond raids, without wading in!

Gillian Fisher

Fierce . . . Whilst Alone

The wildness in his manner was sometimes out of hand,
In fact, he wore his feral streak as if it were a brand,
But because of his immensely cute nose,
I chose not to oppose,
And thus he was allowed to run riot in his land,
But I knew deep down how to take him up in hand.

Sometimes, it seems that he's connected to us by an unseen force,
Because we're attuned to his needs by a few swift calls,
He understands when to resist, he understands when to run,
But he always brings a smile to my face, my little feline son.

The way he chases the birds around like he's playing hide-and-seek,
And the way that he always knows when to make the next frantic leap,
No one knows whether he truly knows his name,
His head sometimes comes up at the call, but mostly he ignores it in vain.

And when he's staking out his territory, he moves like he's a bull mastiff,
But when it comes to back it up, we've found that he's quite passive,
A single scratch and he'd be spent,
He'd sooner run away and spend the week in Kent.
His personality suits more of a midnight saboteur
Oh, and did I mention that his name started with a purr?

To be frankly honest the only place he lavishes any time on,
Other than under the kitchen counters shaking,
Is in his domain, his little nook;
Which of course is my lap, his bed, mistook.

Etta Lararch

The Old Horse

I stand by the gate, my owner I see,
I think of the day when she bought me.
We were both young and headstrong then,
but how many lessons she taught me.
My first canter with her I bucked and I squealed,
my quicksilver hooves seemed to fly.
My speed and my temper I learned to control
and no one was faster than I.

In the show jumping ring the speed of my turns
were usually almost unbeatable.
Opponents would mutter, 'It's him again'
and call me some names unrepeatable.
Two ponytails flying, cross-country we'd go
'Come on good boy', she would cry.
Hedges and ditches were all in my stride
Yes! No one was faster than I.

A new horse arrives and starts to compete,
takes over now I have to rest.
He jumps very well, his performance is good,
My owner still loves me the best.
My cups and rosettes all stand on the shelf,
to win some, he really will try.
Good luck young chap, I hope you have fun,
but never go faster than I.

Now I am old, my legs sometimes stiff,
my hair is dappled with grey,
my best pleasure now, a warm stable at night,
with a good dish of feed and some hay.
Soon I'll be gone where old horses go,
chasing the clouds in the sky
but when I'm remembered they always will say
that no one was faster,
yes, no one was faster,
no one was faster than I.

Jacqueline Longley

22

Mischievous Little Kitty

Mischievous little kitty
Purring with delight when you give him chicken
Squealing when you take him to the vets
Giving you that look which says it all
Almost never in the house, but you don't care - because
When he is -
That little bundle of fur is
Perfect.

Emma Yeo

Nirvana (Our Afghan)

She sits in silence, cocooned in a state of perfect bliss,
Such adoration and beauty, life doesn't get much better than this,
An angel of elegance, embellished in splendour achieved from the soul,
Not for her the beckoning return of a mere mortal's call.

A vision of loveliness with her long shiny hair
Such femininity and sensuality radiating from one so fair
With a sweep of her lashes and a look so demure
This heaven-sent creature exudes all that is pure.

With a graceful gait reminiscent of a model's catwalk,
What words would she say if only she could talk?
This spiritual goddess was she sent from afar?
Not really from Bexleyheath, we collected by car.

We love her to bits, airs, graces and all
And if on occasions from her pedestal she should fall
Her manners not becoming of our gracious queen
We'll look the other way and pretend we have not seen.

Cris Ingham

Patch

What can I say about Patch?
A meddlesome cat, that can lift a latch.
In he sneaks, whenever there is a chance.
No one knows who he belongs to,
No one gives him a second glance.

He eats all in sight, comes back for more at night.
He can be quite peevish, when he does not get his way
This asylum seeker he never goes away.
His best buddy, Molly, is getting quite wary
Patch and his habits can be very scary.

He snaffles the tea and the supper
Moll's owner is beginning to suffer.
The feeding of the five thousand is not exactly sporting
And Moll, if she's honest, is too old for courting.
It's about time the owner took control here

And got his tired brain into gear
Or will he allow complacency to rule?
Because this asylum seeker is no fool.
He has his cake and eats it and Molly he will pester
Bad tempered she is going to get and her mood will fester.

There is only trouble, Patch will stir
And then, won't there be flying fur.

Ellen Spiring

My Lion King

Old Mogadon of Mogadishu sits by my side.
He's black and scruffy; always malting
But with a lion's pride.

From his old fangy mouth, purry complaints emit
Often howly, sometimes prowly.
He's often very sick.

When horizontally poised, he makes little noise.
Soft purr breaths waft the air.
But beware his slumber, his watchful slumber.
With eye half open and nose twitch repose,
He's a peeping Tom in elegant pose.

Battered and unhurried,
He cares not about worries.
Once king of the road from old lion clan,
He's not any old lion; he's my old lion,
He's the king of my divan.

Nicole Touye

Dancing Ostriches

How beautiful they are, the ostrich ladies,
How well sprung and bouncily balanced;
As supermodels they swivel and turn,
Pirouette and sweep on their leathery,
En pointe, hardnail tiptoes.
Their eyes are glossy pools of mischief
Veiled by curtains of feathery lash,
And smiling beaks of rosy ivory horn
In a high-cheekbone sculptured face.
When the dark blue winds bring the rains
Gusts goose the ostrich ladies, like maiden aunts,
Get under their skirts; fill them with skittish glee,
Turn them girlish, flirty, reckless and wild.
How they float on the veldt, how they dance.
See them bend and sway their infinite necks,
Wield their wings like feather fans at the opera,
So flighty you might imagine them aloft,
Filling the Wedgwood clouds with their soft
Grey plumes, their long, incomparable shins
Tucked up under bony chests, or flowing behind,
Long necks outstretched, eyes closed to the breeze,
We might even catch a sparkle of frivolous gems
On each bony brow, or at each furry throat.
'Look at us flying,' they seem to say. 'Look!
If Peter Ilyich had seen us first, he would
Have written a ballet for us, an ostrich opera,
Not those portly waddling swans!'

Liz Davies

Would You Believe It

I have a dog, his name is Gruff,
He's brown and white, and looks really tough.
His skin it wrinkles on his face,
Gruff don't move much, he knows his place.
He sits with front legs wide apart
And once he stole my mum's jam tart!
Well now I got the blame for that
And Gruff just sat there looking fat.
He never ever barks a lot
But then he won't, cos he's made of pot!

Betty Glover

Alfie

Alfie, an agile cat, fancied himself as a fighter,
Always attacking older cats, although was much lighter.
He would run at them from a distance and jump through the air,
They often snarled at him but Alfie did not seem to care.

Of course, his new young owners allowed him far too much leeway,
After he had arrived at their home, a bedraggled stray.
Instantly, he was accepted as a family member,
How long he lived with them, no one could ever remember.

Over years Alfie became stubborn, trait none could deter,
He could best be described as a real character.
But to people he liked, shared his beautiful loving side
Walking around the neighbourhood, head held high with feline pride.

Susan Mullinger

Rusty

Rusty you were my beautiful red setter
No other dog I loved any better
You would rest your head upon my knee
With loving eyes, looking up at me.

We loved you Rusty every day
But sadly you had nowhere to play
So you could have a better life, we had to part
Leaving us who loved you with a broken heart.

Rusty at least you have a good home
With friends, who'll want to share your bone
You'll walk and play together every day
You looked so happy, as you went on your way.

Rusty you gave us pleasure and love too
Though naughty at times, we did love you
Hope you're happy every day
As with your setter friends you play.

We'll never forget you Rusty, our big red
We miss you sharing with us our bed!

Joan Read

The Life Of A Tortoise

She trundles silently across the ground
Moving at her own leisurely pace:
She must wait until the sun shines
Before she can show her face.

Her one love in life is cucumber,
All green and full of juice
Although she is partial to a bit of apple
And sweet cherries at a push!

She must wait until the sun comes out
As she does not enjoy the cold;
She needs a Mediterranean temperature
For someone considered so old

And yet have you ever seen a tortoise move?
So carefree and gentle across the grass.
She may not get a move on
But she always makes us laugh!

Her shell always looks so heavy
And determined she can be.
Especially if there is something in her way:
That 'something' is normally me!

She will come and find us when she's hungry
But she has an attitude too.
Just because she may look sweet
She has a very thick shell too.

We think that she'll outlive us,
She is in a very good state
And yet the sun has to go down one day.
For now, she is content with a grape!

Sarah Buttery

Who? Me?

You glare at me again
With that hard look in your eye
Like you think I understand;
That I know the reason why
Yet other times you tell me
That I haven't got a brain
And you regularly scold me
For being a little pain.

But this smacks of double standards, Mum,
If I may be so bold
And how could I understand
When I'm only six months old?
And when I slip my lead, Mum
To play with other dogs
That's instinct, see, to socialise;
Plus I have to chase those cats and frogs!

But I think you know, cos as ever, Mum
Your resolve begins to crack
Works every time, those floppy paws,
Whilst lying on my back
And you know as well as I do
That by ten o'clock tonight
I'll be cradled in your arms
Watching films by candlelight.

So, I know I chewed your shoe, Mum,
And I know I ate your mat
But I haven't got a brain, Mum -
Had you not remembered that?

Andrew Beardmore

Misty

I have a little cat, Misty is her name
She knows all the tricks, how to play the game
Of getting her wishes granted, just like a dame
Who knows exactly what she wants, then more of the same.

She's not selfish, you know, just for luxury she pines
No Whiskas for her, only prawns when she dines
If milk were to be rationed, she would have the best off the vines
And if cats wore clothes, she would be dressed to the nines.

She's the apple of my eye, though she treats me like a slave
And really hasn't a clue, on how to behave
When my friends come calling, she has no faith
But bolts for the door, to disappear like a wraith.

When summer comes, she loves the outdoor
But when winter's here, she hogs the floor
And woe betide anyone, who opens the door
For spoiling her siesta, her scorn she will pour.

The times you are low, on your lap she will climb,
Sharing your sorrows, for quite a long time
But spoiling your clothes, with a residue of grime
Knowing her purring, will assuage any crime.

She's a little madam, who can show some disdain
When her dignity is threatened, her anger is plain
But mostly, she makes you smile, with her antics to gain
Your undying love and sure shelter from rain.

But Misty now, has her home to share
With two other moggies, who needed a lair
She was not very happy, and retreated upstair
But gradually she's accepting, it's time to share.

So now this threesome, though different as can be
Are learning to think, and say, 'after me'
For to share is good, they are beginning to see
Allowing them to live, in agreed harmony.

Margaret Webster Thomson

And The Boats Sing

Pastel coloured, plastered four storey beach front houses
Windows watching the sea through elegant panes
As the anchored boats sing in the wind and rain
Small blue jackdaw eyes are watching as gulls swoop and fly amongst the
cars, scavenging
Precarious landing on tall chimneys, high vantage points for the all-seeing
gulls
Large black rainclouds gather as a pair of long fluffy grey ears in a rice
trailer passes by
No one likes to ride donkeys in the rain, so home for tea
And still the boats sing
Whilst flags, flop and flap and riggings on the pulled up boats
Clank, clank, clank metal on metal, against the screeching of the gulls

Jackdaws wait whilst lamp posts sway in the strong winds
Sun breaks through the storm clouds
Reflecting the houses and cars in the deep puddles
The birds preen as if in a mirror
And still the boats sing
Squabbles erupt as food is found
Dominating gulls yet the smaller jackdaws still find rich pickings
Beaks are cleaned on windswept tree branches
Lame gull waits as jackdaws throw rubbish from inside the litter bin
Three jackdaws inside and one on lookout and an orderly line of jackdaws
waiting -
A definite pecking order
And still the boats continue to sing to the scavengers.

Hilary Jean Clark

Cat's-Eye View

Pussy pussy
Warm and dry
Let the world
Pass on by
Snowflakes falling
Thick and fast
The morning sun
Did not last
Behind the trees
Whose web-like branches
Tower the little firs
Trees that glitter
Twinkling lights
Holly berries -
Round the bin
Keep the cold outside
Where it belongs
Let there be warmth
Within.

Irene Grant

Wonderfully Sly

Sitting staring, mostly caring
mouth so full, as the prawn aroma lingers,
big black circles focused (on the dish),
another mouthful forced down.

Empty.

Lying slowly in the window sill
a paw outstretched wipes away the mess.
Too lazy to continue, the tail rests playfully over the sill.
Another meal ends, wonder when the next will come.

Climbing heavily up the stairs,
he inquisitively wanders into the room.
idle paws a merge onto the edge,
bumpy, chunky and noisy he crawls across the bed.

Cosy on top of the covers,
a damp face pressed against an arm,
the broken nose edging ever closer,
body heat transferring from me to him.

Pushing me onto the floor
this little fuzzy creature
that we call Baby.

Gemma Mountain

Marmalade

When protecting your domain
A fireball of ginger fur,
Or a feline fluffy mass
With paddy paws and purr.
A sandy piece of fluff,
A two-tone coloured cat,
Adopted as a kitten,
Now lounging on my mat.
A selfish piece of warmth,
Projecting a selfless love,
But if you should be disturbed
You'd soon leave home or move!

Joan Elizabeth Blissett

What's My Line?

Open day a group of canines met, and they began to speak
Of all the clever things they did to earn their board and keep.
'Let's take turns,' a gundog cried, 'I'll be the first to start.'
At this, with a yawn, a chow sat down, a little way apart.

'I raise the birds,' the gundog said, 'and flush them from the heather,
I'm highly skilled and take great care not to hurt a single feather.'
'It's such great fun to race around, then flop down whilst they're firing.'
'It might be fun,' the chow-chow said, 'but don't you find it tiring?'

'I do cartwheels,' the poodle said, 'and balance on one leg,
And chase my tail and give a paw and then sit up to beg.'
'It's such a shame,' the chow chow said, 'when his talent's undeniable,
That he behaves in such a way. I think he's certifiable!'

'I round up ewes,' the sheepdog said, 'around the hills and glens,
Then run them home and sort them out, into their different pens.'
'Sometimes,' he said, 'I have to work from dawn till dusk each day.'
'Well, don't tell me,' the chow chow said, 'tell the RSPCA.'

'I'm with the police,' the Alsatian said. 'it's a grand life in the force.'
'But dangerous,' the chow chow said, 'you realise that of course?'
'Police dogs are brave,' the Alsatian said, 'they chase off thieves
                                              and muggers.'
'If you ask me,' the chow chow said, 'police dogs are silly - animals!'

'My master's blind,' the Labrador said, 'so he depends on me
To take him where he wants to go, wherever that may be.'
'Well really now,' the chow chow said, 'most praiseworthy I'm sure
No doubt you do a splendid job, but what a frightful bore.'

'Well, what's your line?' the dogs all cried. 'So what do you do, Chow?
We've told you all about ourselves. Come on, it's your turn now.'
'You want to know just what I do?' the chow stretched out at ease.
'I'll tell you then, here's what I do, exactly what I please!'

Molly Mettam

Hippy Happy Hamster

Bibby is what we call her
A name created by a toddler
Honey mixed with caramel
Is the colour of her fur.

Beady little eyes
Sit upon her face
She runs so fast
I'm sure she could win a race!

She may only be small
But small is cute
Though sometimes when she's noisy
I wish she had a mute.

Bibby, bobby, babby
Hippy, hoppy, happy
That's her alright.

Bianka Hannam (14)

For A Walk

I hear the lead and know it's time
To take a walk in the nice sunshine
Out we go and down the road
But something says, this is not right
The fields and park nowhere in sight.

I plod along my head held low
And get this feeling I don't want to go
What is it that makes me feel this way?
I really thought we were out to play
No, let's go home, something's not quite right
The lead is held a bit too tight.

We're walking on a bit too fast
How long is this feeling going to last?
Not even time to sniff the grass
Then suddenly I know we're there
There's a nasty smell about the air
Then I'm up some steps and through the door
And made to sit upon the floor.
It can't get worse I tell myself
I know I'm in the best of health
But I know it's going to get worse yet
I'm here to see that nasty vet!

Hazel Webb

Our Puss

Down among the rushes
Beside the torrent's edge
In darkest suit, pale mitts and tie
Intrepid steps and furtive eye
I spied our fearsome puss.

He would not look at me at all
His gaze was steely still
He thought of far more serious things
Like whom he'd like to kill!

Rosemary Keith

William The Spider

William the spider lives upstairs
He peeps out at me when I say my prayers
Sits on the curtain as I read my book
Then scurries away to his secret nook
I want William the spider to be my friend
With his bright little eyes and legs all bent
He could come to my party for then I'll be four
Or play hide-and-seek with my toys on the floor
But William the spider is so very shy
He hides under the bed if I walk by
I close the door gently if I scare him you see
He may just move house and leave me sad as can be.

Doreen Goodway

Cats Are Me

Nobody to talk to
Nobody to love
Sitting by yourself with a new TV.

Go to work with others
Got to pay the bills
Chat about their problems and the old TV.

Finish with the shopping
Haul it to the car
Going to miss that programme on the damn TV.

Open up the front door -
Loving, furry faces -
Jacob, Tim and Little 'Un mean all the world to me!

Lilian Perriman

In Memory Of Millie

My Millie so cute, so sweet
No longer with me
Such a lonely feat.

Her beautiful presence
Eyes so bright
Little paws that scratch at my door at night.

Trails of fur behind, she did leave
Leaving me here alone to grieve
Sometimes I hear her
Little cries in the night
Why, oh why, did she have to die?

I know in my heart
That she is now at peace
In cat Heaven
Having a feast.

With all your pals
I bet you play
Running through fields
Happy and gay.

Millie, my Millie
I will never forget
What a joy you were
A fantastic pet.

Peace be with you
These tears I shed
My little companion
You are not really dead.

Your spirit lives on
I miss you so
But I know with fondness
You wanted to go.

Your time on Earth
Was wisely spent
Chasing mice and prey
A funny event.

Goodbye my Millie
I wish you well
Have fun in Cat Land
Sweet dreams
Farewell.

Juliette Anne Foulger

Milly

My daughter has a lovely dog, her name is Milly
She's cute and funny and sometimes so silly.
She's always hiding food . . . here and there
Bonio in the shower . . . chews on the chair.
Milly is very small so she doesn't eat a lot
But certainly wants to keep all the food she's got.
She hides it from my dog Cariad, her best friend
Who always sniffs it out and finds it in the end.
Cariad eats what she's found . . . not guilty at all
She thinks . . . she found it and that's a fair call.
Milly then gets annoyed, growls and snaps
Then as quick as can be jumps onto our laps.
Milly is a cross Pom . . . fluffy and small,
Cariad a German shepherd . . . slim and tall.
They're the best of pals and cuddle up together
Leaving lots of dog hair on my sofa . . . it's leather!
Milly is young and busy . . . not yet three
Cariad is nearly ten . . . it makes a difference you see,
Because Milly always wants to run and play
But Cariad gets tired by the end of the day.
Although Milly's the youngest she's definitely the boss
But Cariad's so gentle and kind . . . to her it's no loss.
Having two such lovely dogs . . . we're lucky indeed
Such different characters because of their different breed.
Cariad's a lady . . . cool, calm, classy and sleek
While Milly is busy . . . nosy, bossy and full of cheek!

Enfys Evans

Fun With Fudge

Fudge is my name, so I am told,
I love my owner, rarely am I bold.
Times I'm in trouble I do not savour
When really, I'm on my best behaviour.

I like to climb the stairs,
The tables and the chairs,
But her shoulder is my perch,
There I worship like a church.

I see the house at work
And smell leftovers, a great perk.
While everyone's out during the light
I sleep away napping through my night.

During their night, my day,
On my wheel I play,
I rush about, nibbling and storing
Gnawing while the house is snoring.

I love cuddles, given frequently,
And kisses received regularly.
In return I listen to tears,
Secret tales and fears.

I'm a world-class artist, a regular Houdini,
I can twist and wriggle, even if I'm teeny.
Fudge is my name, so I am told,
I'm loved in this family fold.
My brown body is furry
And on my paws I scurry.
I have a white chest
And I'm a hamster, the world's best!

Caitríona O'Brien

Chipped

Well just fancy that, I'm a microchipped cat,
So I'm 121,736,674 A,
But I'd still be just Dandy if I had my way.
I've now joined the age of the modern computer;
The vet got me under my skin with his shooter.
Though I tried to resist with my teeth and my paws,
There was no one in reach of my dangerous claws.
I was shamelessly grabbed by the scruff of my neck,
And brought willy-nilly to a state of high tech.
If anyone dare shout my microchip number;
With eyes tightly shut, I'll continue to slumber.
Being a number's an undignified bore, say
I. Who's 121,736,674 - A?

Janet Lang

New Found Friend

Sat on a bench, in the park one day,
I fell for her in a heavy way.
She touched my arm,
She was gentle and warm,
Her coat looked good,
She oozed with grace,
Her breath was hot as she licked my face,
She was a loner; I'd seen her before,
She followed me home, and sat by my door.
I waited a while, then invited her in,
I gave her some refreshment,
In a biscuit tin.
It now seems ages since I met my stray,
But the dog is still with me even today.

A T Lammiman

The Vital Message

Buster, the boxer, loved to chew
from Dad's best slippers, to leftover stew.
He'd nibble the carpet, when he got bored,
and then have a go at the skirting board.

Everything had to be hidden from sight,
when Buster was alone, by day or by night.
But one day, while Father was making some toast
Buster devoured the morning post.
What vital letter had come through the door?
For parts of the jigsaw, lay wet on the floor.

So it took Dad till almost the end of the day,
to join up the letter and what did it say?
Well, it wasn't a letter, but a flyer (quite rare),
from a house alarm company, with an ironic flair.

It was cut in the shape of a burglar called Bert,
with bandana and swag bag, and stripy T-shirt.
Saying, 'Think how easy it might possibly be
for a real burglar to enter as easy as me!'

Margaret Sanderson

Dog

Every dog must have its day
Or so they used to say.
It's so stupid, so inane,
When so many try in vain
To beg, to plead, just to be part
Of a family or someone's heart.

Puppies are fun, puppies are sweet,
Puppies grow up, get under the feet.
But they don't deserve that kick,
Just a firm word will earn a loving lick.

Dogs left or cast out,
That's what a dog's home is all about.
They do their best to care for all
For the many that wait a master's call.

Gazing at the door with soft brown eyes,
Hoping they don't mean those goodbyes.
Folk who petted, cuddled, then cast aside,
How could you do it? How could you abide
To be so cruel to one who sat by your side?

If you've a dog, love it, keep it safe,
Don't let it be a furry waif.
Remember it gave you its heart,
If you turn away you'll tear it apart.

Ruth Allerston

Puppies At Play

When puppy dogs play they can bounce all around
So rarely do they have four feet on the ground
In fact it's no wonder that sometimes they fall
As often they're standing on no feet at all

Not yet too sure of what's up and what's down
Their tumbling skills could out do any clown
They roll and do cartwheels then look so confused
Yet cleverly managing not to get bruised

And what about flowers they must be fun too
As well as a good place to go to the loo
They sniff at the petals which tickle their noses
Then bite off the heads of those tasty prize roses

Then there's what happens when they meet a slope
Now this is a time when they really can't cope
One minute they're walking their head held up high
The very next second they're staring at sky

Then all of a sudden whilst chasing their tails
The thing that produces their energy fails
Instantly sleeping as they hit the floor
They're dreaming of playing and bouncing some more.

Cheryl Lucas

Cyril The Friendly Squirrel

A squirrel from its oak tree
Went speeding down the road,
A camera flashed and caught him
Not obeying the Highway Code.
At thirty-seven miles per hour
So fleet of foot was he,
That astonished police now saw him
Not in his favourite tree.
Now Cyril turned detective
To make up for that jaunt
He led a policeman to stolen goods
At the base of his tree to flaunt.
So squirrels can be helpful
And not against the law
They're loving, friendly creatures
Our friends for evermore.

Valma June Streatfield

Our Peppi

A black and tan tiny dog, a Yorkshire Terrier his breed,
Adored by the family, a special pet, Fiona's need.
She had him as a puppy; he rode home on her lap,
Bounding through the door, it was then he saw the cat.
With patience they became good mates
The cockatiel and rabbits too,
Two children made the family group, happiness shone through.
Just a few years of a very charmed life,
His joints caused some concern,
Until one day his spine gave out, then we had a lot to learn.
No treatment by the vet, could help our little friend,
He went to sleep in dogland, God's creatures, he would only lend.
We often talk of Peppi, so lively, good and clever,
We look at pictures of his handsome looks
And will love this friend forever.

Patricia Evans

Winner Takes All

A funny thing happened the other morn
I looked out of the window, on the lawn
Sat a woodpigeon, puffed up full of fight
Guarding some bread that was his by right.

A grey squirrel was circling the bird
I took in the scene, it was quite absurd
To watch the squirrel narrowing the distance
And the pigeon trying to maintain its stance.

The bird got quite nervous as the squirrel neared
To lose its prize it greatly feared.
I watched with ever greater interest
Who would come top in this unequal contest?

The pigeon's squawk was not of defeat
It told the squirrel it ought to retreat.
But the little grey took a jump instead
And ran away with the coveted bread!

Lisa Wolfe

The Puppy And The Mouse

The puppy was rather manic,
he ran around in a panic,
a mouse ran by making him squeal,
but it wasn't even real.

What was this thing running around,
is it fun or out of bounds,
too young to understand the ways of life yet,
the poor little puppy began to fret.

In time he began to see,
how much fun this new toy could be,
running around having fun,
oops, he's eaten it, now he has a full tum!

Julie Marie Laura Shearing

The Black Widow

The black widow is motionless
Upon her silken silver web
Watches, waits, for her prey to come
He arrives and sees the Devil's daughter
The next hours are filled with fertility.

Soon the male's death package arrives
In the dark she pounces like a vampire
Inflicting the love bite of death on him
A body on a beautiful web spoiling its nature
She drops it willingly and moves away.

Her children like drops of Venus' product
Soon they will grow to be like her
Vicious, blood-thirsty predators
Motionless upon their silken silver webs
There is no death for a black widow.

Tarandeep Sandhar

Cats

They ran from here to there and back,
Grey flashed past, then black and white.
Through this room, around a chair,
Then back they came, still in our sight,
Then through the kitchen, round its table,
Over chairs and on their way.
All three were the best of friends
So really it was only play.
When they got back they were quite tired
And the female jumped up top
Others just fell on the floor
And there they all flaked out, kerplop!

Veryan Eldridge

Pat The Dog

Now Pat she was a lovely dog,
She belonged to where I worked,
Her owners were lord of the manor
To her they were her king and queen.

One day they asked if my husband and I
Would stay in the house for two nights
To look after Pat the dog and to feed her
And to see that she was all right.

They arranged for another employee to take her
Out for a walk each day
But we were the boss in her own eyes
And he could not take her away.

On the morning they were due to arrive back home
I heard them drive into the yard
I told Pat her master was here
And she rushed out very hard.

She met them as they got out of the car
And her expression said, where have you been?
We were no longer the boss of her home
As the last two days we had been.

She was getting older and very weak
She often struggled to walk
But she found new energy to welcome them back
And we almost felt she could talk.

Iris Covell

A Dog's Plea

I look up with hopeful and pleading eyes,
I wag my tail but inside, my heart cries.
Please, look at me, don't pass me by,
I'm so alone and afraid, and I don't want to die.
I didn't do anything wrong and I'm not bad,
But nobody loves me, that's why I'm so sad.
I wish you would take me home with you,
My shattered faith in humans to renew.
I know it's not your fault, you're not to blame,
But for thousands of dogs to die unloved is a shame!
Please, look within me to my faithful heart,
In a body so bruised and torn apart.
Yet still I could learn to trust once more,
To be a happy dog with a future in store.
Just give me your love, a warm bed and some food,
In return I will love you and always be good.
I'd be so content, just to lie at your feet,
A better friend than me, you could never meet.

So if one day, in a dog's home you see,
A plain old dog, please hear my plea.
Don't pass him by without a second glance
Don't walk away, please give him a chance.
He may not be pretty or have a pedigree
But that sad plain old dog might just be me.

Maureen Roberts

Best Friends?

Dozing on an autumn day
On the doorstep Topsy lay.
Her tummy full and quite content,
When suddenly the air was rent
With the seagulls raucous call -
It really wasn't fair at all.
Her ears she covered with her paws
For she knew Quacker wouldn't pause
In her attempt to wake the cat.
She'd come for food, and that was that.
'Oh go away you silly bird
The noise you make is quite absurd.'
'I want my dinner,' Quacker said,
'And I know you have just been fed.'
'Hard luck,' said Puss, 'none left today -
Now let me sleep - please go away.'
Quacker stamped his feet upon the lawn,
Up popped an unsuspecting worm.
'A tasty morsel,' Quacker said,
And lifting up his snow-white head
And squawking his triumph did declare
To all things flying in the air.
Poor Topsy said, 'I wish, I wish
You'd go and catch yourself a fish.'
But Quacker thought the worm great fun,
And stamped and caught another one.
Again she squawked in sheer delight
Putting all the little birds to flight.
But worms were saltier things than fish
She'd have a drink from Topsy's dish.
Topsy was having none of that
Quacks was a bird and she a cat.
So creeping up, she pounced upon her friend
Oh, surely this was not the end.
That wily bird, away she flew
She knew precisely what to do.
'Missed me,' she screeched to Puss in glee,
'Enjoy your sleep; I'll be back for tea!'

Barbara Dunning

Meeting Mr Mousy

Mr Mousy resides at the King's Cross tube railway.
Last night around eleven at night,
I met Mr Mousy while he was munching discarded crisps.
Our eyes met,
Mr Mousy moved quickly along the platform wall a bit
Then posed motionless.
He was looking back at me from the corners of his eyes
His backside towards me.
I felt like a rude neighbour,
Who invites herself to a next-door's kitchen.
I quickly pretended everything was fine,
Mr Mousy acknowledged my apology and continued to munch.
But it lasted only a minute
The tube approached with gushing wind.
Mr Mousy ignored the mechanical disturbance
Which vibrated the whole of the tunnel.
I put one foot forward to get ready for the arriving tube
As I lifted my foot Mr Mousy dashed towards a rail and disappeared in
                                                        the dark.
The carriages rolled in just as Mr Mousy excused himself from the platform.
What amazing timing. How does he do it?
'Goodbye Mr Mousy, you are swell.'

Yoko Hand

Hawk And Doves

You sit on the fence, eyes full of hunger
Body skeletal but majestic
Once revered by ancient peoples
Your presence even during
A famine a powerful one.

A predator
Searching
Whilst the
Victims are
Static, fearsome
They will
Meet the
Fate their
Sibling did
Only hours earlier.

Prey a
Symbol of
Peace
To humans
But to you
Much needed
Nourishment
You depart
   Unsuccessful this time
      But you
         Will return.

Gaelynne Pound

Odd Animals And Crawly Things

I'm a lizard
Hunting food at which I'm a wizard
I lie in the heat until I'm replete
After my prey has gone down my gizzard.

I'm a sloth
I hang upside down by my toethe
But that's how I was made; I'm so sad and afraid
Cos it's something I hate and I loathe.

I'm a giraffe
Tallest of all by a half
I'm ungainly and slow when I get vertigo
Well, it's always good for a laugh.

I'm an aardvark
I was given this name for a lark
My personality's low and my mind's rather slow
So I prefer to stay in the dark.

I'm a toad
Which is hazardous when crossing the road
So I stay by my pond of which I am fond
Which is where my intelligence shoad.

I'm a hyena
Believe me there's no animal that's meaner
I forage and sup, eating everything up
So there's no need for a vacuum cleaner.

I'm a bat
An odd looking thing but that's that
So just ask my spouse when I'm called flying mouse
She prefers that to me being called rat.

I'm a gnu
Now that's got you in a bit of a stew
Is the 'G' silent like gnat, the answer to that
Is in the animals' who's who in the zoo.

Peter Colenutt

Dogs

Some become such beloved pets
Small, large, shaggy coats, smoothed
Still at times they will all need vets
Keeping them healthy, their ailments soothed.

So why not visit an animal shelter
Such woebegone faces, different furs
Unwanted pups, ousted, helter-skelter
Often dumped, these different colour curs.

Why do humans have to be so unkind?
To punish a present, that's become a pest
Take one home; open the goodness of your mind
Make one little orphan who might be ugly, find rest.

Marjorie Busby

Blacky's Christmas Animal Crackers

It gets harder for a feline
To understand the human race,
Especially at Christmas
When they clutter up the place.

Trimmings, stockings, fairy lights
Presents and a tree,
If they don't cease this nonsense soon
There won't be room for me!

Cakes and puddings are the rule
All things that make them fat,
Plus, they always buy a turkey
Now I don't mind a bit of that.

Later on at party time
They all wear a Christmas hat,
If that's what it takes for a present
Well, I'll go along with that!

But hang on, just a minute
There isn't one for me,
I'll have to pinch one off the dog
Whilst she's spark out 'neath the tree!

Bell Ferris

Cantabile

Most birds are born
with a flair for chorusing dawn.
They rehearse by themselves
in their eggshells.

Once on Earth
having cracked birth,
they're soon vying
with one another at flying.

Once done, all summer
under the eaves their feathered number
are footloose to foster musical skills,
practising mordents and trills.

Rosemary Benzing

Feline Grace

Cats are nimble
Cats are fast
Cats can jump
Cats can spring past
Cats
Cats love to hunt
Cats like to listen
Cats love to sully
The splendour of the mouse
The insect, the sparrow
Cats
Cats can relax
Cats can linger
Cats can stretch
Roll and purr
Can sleep and slumber
Cats
Cars are courageous
Cats are athletic
Cats can climb
Can claw and pierce
Cats can surprise
And tame a tree
Cats.

Margaret Bennett

With Misty And With Skye

If I go down to the river, to paddle in the stream,
Watch the minnows, dangle my tootsies, sit as in a dream;
Then let me go with favourite friends, as on the banks we lie,
Let me go with my two Jack Russells - with Misty and with Skye.

Let us run in summer sun with azure overhead,
In forests filled with pine trees, with scorched grass for a bed;
And let me breathe, with gulps of air, the scent of flowers dry,
To smell their perfume with my two Jack Russells - with Misty and with
Skye.

To watch the curlew and other birds, circling on the wing,
The sweet delight of Mother Nature as she begins to sing;
The breaking waves on sandy shore, the billows swelling high,
Let me run with my two Jack Russells - with Misty and with Skye.

Loveliness cannot last forever, nor even life alone,
We are as players on the stage and soon we are called home;
When summer goes and autumn comes and leaves begin to die,
Then let me die with my beloved Jack Russells - with Misty and with Skye.

Joyce C Langlands

Next-Door's Cat

Black as night
Eyes so bright
They can be seen in the dark
A coat of velvet
Kept so clean and neat
Can be so gentle
And so meek.
It moves so gracefully
And looks so sleek
But underneath a killer lurks
As it pounces with
Those deadly claws
Birds that fly
Mouse or rat
Are not safe from that old cat.

Betty Middlemist

Are Dogs Human?

I wag my tail when I am happy
And bark but cannot talk
But I know the looks that will ask you
Can we please go for a walk?

I know I ate your camera
And tore up that big box of tissues
But when you took this dog along
You also adopted issues.

I will love you when you're happy
And I will love when you're scared
But if you bellow out your anger
I may piddle on your stairs!

I'm only a dog when all is said and done
And I'm sometimes a bit of a brute
But when you see me in my basket
I know you think I'm cute

So are dogs at all human?
Well, sometimes we think we are
But dogs are what God made us
And dogs are much better by far.

Linda Coles

Cat And Mouse

Pussycat red, pussycat blue
This little pussycat wants to eat you
Little mouse yellow, little mouse green
This little mouse doesn't want to be seen.

Pussycat black, pussycat white
This little puss will wait all night
Little mouse orange, little mouse brown
Has escaped in a cab and fled into town.

Rodger Moir

For The Love Of Cavaliers

A cavalier obsessive
Is what they label me,
I wish I had all four of them
Right now, there's only three.
Lilly is a Tri-colour
With the softest silky ears,
Penny is a Blenheim
Her antics leave me in tears.
Then there's little Charlie Beau
The cutest Ruby boy,
He'd rather chew my fingers
Than his chewy puppy toy.
Soon I'll have a black and tan
Then I'll have the set,
Please don't tell my husband
I haven't told him yet!
King Charles himself had lots of them
And a special one called Fubs.
I want at least fifteen of them
A football team plus subs!
A cavalier obsessive
Is what they label me,
I wish I had hundreds of them
But for now there's only three!

Julia Fletcher

Mo Chara

My dog's called Mucker
as in trucker
from the Irish mo chara
as in mascara
meaning my friend
we thought it was a really original name
but it's driving us all round the bend.

Every time I call his name
in the street
people just stop and think it's great
that I'm greeting them.

They're smiling and waving
with their hands in the air
I stand and wave back
not wanting to stare
feeling kinda stupid while
impatiently waiting for Mucker
to appear
to take the bad look off me.

Hi Mucker come here!
Mucker get there!
Guaranteed to turn heads
everywhere.

Until one and all
they finally see
my old black and white mongrel
taking a pee on a lamp post.

Then the penny drops
they hurry away
still on three legs
Mucker piddles away
what can I say?
(he does this ten times a day!)

But he's not a bad old dog
sniffing his way
with his big boogly eyes
he's happy and gay.

So think hard
before giving your dog a name
or you'll end up like me
and they'll think you're insane
These strangers you're calling to
and making friends
every walk is the same
and it never ends.

Kevin Meehan

My Cat

My cat is special
Because he is mine,
My cat is hilarious
Most of the time.

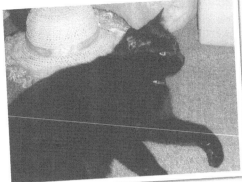

She is completely black
With eyes the colour of the sun.
I really, really love her
But she can be a pain in the bum!

My cat is getting old
She is one year older than me
She was the first to know I was going to be born
She was with my mum at the time you see.

She is loved by the whole family
There are five of us altogether.
I wish she could stay with me
Forever and ever and ever.

Whenever I am ill
Or feeling really sad.
She comes to me with great concern
And she makes me feel really glad.

She is soft when you stroke her
She likes a good tickle
When she fights with our other cat
She gets in a right pickle.

My cat has had four kittens
Two girls and two boys
She loves lots of fuss
And that's the bit she really enjoys.

I love my cat
And nothing in the world will ever change that.

Ellie Bridgwater

Thank You

(Dedicated to Toby the West Highland White Terrier)

The insignificance of a marriage dissolved,
Facing a lifetime alone after so long together,
An empty house now just wraps trinkets and things
Of years built up for a future forever.

Then there's you, a bundle of unconditional adoration
With the natural ability to lift up my heart.
Seven years of cuddly supposedly white perfection,
A custody war just waiting to start!

A TV, a car, no longer important
But your life, your presence, everyone craves.
It's as if desolation was desperately calling
But the life of his owner a Westie he saves!

When the walls were crumbling and the mountains seemed higher,
When insecurities threatened and friends seemed so few,
You brought me your toys and covered me with kisses,
You gave me perception, focus and view.

I now look at the world and everything in it.
Through the eyes of a Westie just wanting to give,
That little bit more to those that adore him,
Ensuring their strength to go out and live!

Claire Morris

Petal

This poem is not about an ordinary cat
This poem is about my cat
My cat called Petal
Or the nickname my dad gave her, Garfield
'Cause she ate so much
And had similar markings
Even though she was a tabby cat.

This is no ordinary cat
This cat could stare at you
Until you gave her what she wanted
This cat knew what she wanted
She wants that mince beef
And she knows you will give it to her
In the end.

This is no ordinary cat
This cat would be in her cat litter tray
For twenty minutes
We all thought she was digging her way to Australia
She never made it there mind you
I found her laying in there once
She's afraid of my hairdryer.

This is no ordinary cat
This cat was a cool cat, a rocker cat
She would be sleeping
I would be listening to loud music like Nickelback
She wouldn't even move
My mum thought she might be deaf
But she could hear me calling her name to give her food pretty well.

This cat is no ordinary cat
This cat knew how to have fun
Even if it meant keeping me awake at night
Throwing her toy around like it was a piece of meat
Or even her running around my room after her ball
Like a footballer on the pitch
She could give them footballers a run for their money.

This cat is no ordinary cat
This cat is my cat called Petal
The one my mum calls Bonsai Tree
The one my dad calls Garfield
Well, all I know is she is my cat Petal
And we will all miss her dearly.

Nadia Williams

Little Miss

Panjenka's dead, now passed away,
still warm in that shoebox tucked away in that bigger
one, once belonging to a pressure cooker.

Wrapped in blankets, her feet, paws,
bent red rose heads tucked between her limbs.

Dad's digging a grave near the plum tree
where no other animals have been put to dust.
Stones mar the unearthing, roots of some tree.

Ma talks to my sister about that flower creeping out
from between the cracks in the wall.

I picture it stretching,
before some hand reaches in and cuts it out.

We stroke her, then watch as she's taken from the vessel
the bursting box lain in the ground.

Three-feet under.
Does that mean she's half a human?
I tell my sister to close Pan's eyes,
that Panjenka is staring. I think to myself
I'd hate for her to be looking at the dirt fall around her.

I stroke her, briefly, then watch her as soil falls
filling around that little broken cat
each person, a spade of dirt.
I jostle with mine and it spills on the green of the grass
where she had lain earlier.

Afterwards, when she's disappeared,
we lay the turf over her tomb,
picture the roots of a tree we intend to plant,
stretch and cradle around her bones.
Little skeleton without the skin.

Ma lays a glass jar which had held tahini
sauce, instead with water and roses, at the tail
of her grave.
Now we sup gin and tonic
without Panjenka needing to feed.

M R Wallis

Henry And Kimba

Two old cats,
both cross
and cranky

decided to get
a little pranky.

So Henry took
Kimba's bell
and bow -

and Kimba took
Henry's hanky!

The fur flew
as they fought
it out

(and I honestly thought
they'd never sort
it out).

But when it was over,
those fine cats
of mine

both jumped on my lap
and sang
Auld Lang Syne!

Maree Teychenné

Joey

He gives me such joy
That bird in a cage
Such a small creature
Whose chirp's no longer strange

He's the light of my life
But has a mind of his own
He's sometimes naughty
And my voice is my own.

He throws out his seed to my dismay
Then looks at me as if just to say
I'll do it again, you just watch
I know you don't like it but thanks very much.

He plays with his toys
And twists on his swing
Then rings his bell
Ding-a-ling-a-ling!

He is so clever and amusing too
When I say twiddle two mirrors he'll do
They both spin around, this toy he just loves
With mirrors attached, he'll play round and above.

I love my Joey, he lightens my life
Others adore him his plumage so bright
Blue and white feathers, he's clever and pretty
That is the reason I've written this ditty.

Andrea Lynne Taylor

The Rock Cat

Who can jump like you?
Who can run like you?
You can my Napoleon
You lived in all seasons
Watching our silly fashions
And glam-rock ideas

Now, we are all grown up
With family of our own
You are gone but not forgotten
That's why I'm putting you in a book
To save the world and set us free
You get the rock cats medal of bravery.

Kenneth Mood

Tortoise

A tortoise may seem a strange pet to buy
I endured scorn from family and friends
A tortoise! What for and why?

You can't take it for walks or cuddle it when feeling blue
and isn't it weird to have a pet
that will outlive you?

Okay, okay, a tortoise is a strange pet to keep
but I love my tortoise even if it doesn't spend
three months a year, well, asleep.

My tortoise is a curiosity when people visit my house,
My window cleaner did wonder where was
the rear and was the mouth.

'It doesn't move very fast,' my father said with come conceit,
but surely movement is a relative thing
and anyway you could use my pet as a seat.

You can't dismiss something for being too slow
British Rail and the Royal Mail make my tortoise
look like Carl Lewis when someone shouts go!

'Life is a marathon not a sprint,' a philosopher might say,
you will not see a tortoise having Botox
or fend off the rigours of time and decay.

I love my tortoise, its crinkled neck and dark sullen eyes,
it's beautiful and graceful and
a mere teenager at seventy-five.

Howard Fairey

Rehabilitation

Given to study, how much can we dare
Give rein to imagination of creatures in despair.
Situations with humour, where we can be of avail,
Naming Bob the Builder with an adder in a pail.
Incidents proving knowledge of animal care,
Underlying danger, yet being totally aware.
That with our help and experience today,
We can set them free to go on their way.
All this, basically from serious study now,
Proves to show that we really did learn how.

Betty Bukall

Arabian Horses

Spicy aroma of the east fairy tales
Fills charming image of the Arabian mares.
Beautiful legend as halo to mystery
Surrounds these divine creature in history.
Picturesque lines of the ideal body
Attractive as dawning - golden and ruddy.
Sunbeams deftly plaited in mane . . .
In sparkling glance - is spilt 'starry grain'.

An ultimate achievement of nature,
A mature and perfect creature.
An intuitive soul, an intelligent spirit
The noble beauty, hallmark of merit.

Lena V Chyzh

Puzzle

Annoyance rising from your feet slowly,
The creaking of the back door.
Raising it past your knees,
Eyes feasting on the sight,
Mud scattered across the once sparkling floor.

Small footprints formed in brown liquid,
The anger hits your hips,
The owner of these pawprints
Causes a load of clattering upstairs.
Ears ringing at the sound
Your favourite vase, maybe?

Mud patterns repeated over and over,
Across the hallway - up the stairs.
Climbing the stair,
Annoyance hits your shoulders,
As your footing if jolted by the slippery surface.

Turning the corner, anger in your head
Mouth open, ready to shout . . .
You find your adorable rough collie
Muddy and wrapped up in your new duvet.

Your heart melts, the anger's gone.

Laura Ford

The Tilly Cat

Her purr is one of pleasure -
a message of her love -
she stares at me with bright green eyes,
and I can't help but smile.

She's there for me from dawn 'til dusk,
stretched out across our bed.
She likes it when I pet her head,
her halo of silky coal,
and she'll snuggle closer, closer yet,
and the world will slip away.

I've never known a cat like her,
one who's with me all the time.
She even joins me in the bath
and sits between the taps!

Her loyalty is humbling,
for she never does get mad.
She's stuck with me through thick and thin,
a really special gift.
I will never have another friend,
as bound as she and I.

She lies with me, even now,
her head against my lap.
She looks at me and I know that
I love her so much back.

Ria Landrygan

Jack, You're Always Here

(I would like to dedicate this poem to my dog Jack who sadly passed away)

It would be cool if you talked
And cool if you danced
But I liked the way you were

It would be cool if you walked on two legs
And cool if you wore kegs
But I liked the way you were

You dug holes at the beach
And never liked quiche
But I liked the way you were

Now you're gone it's really hard
But I know you're always here
Looking down on all the family
I close my eyes and you are near.

Megan Eve Cook

Taylor

Woops!
Sorry
I didn't know you were there
Even though you follow me everywhere
I'm so sorry I do really care
You should have been called Shadow
Every time I turn around you are there
Still it's nice really
Cos I know you care
Your bark is worse than your bite
You sleep by my bed at night
We have some wonderful walks out together
No matter what kind of weather
It's wearing down my shoe leather
But I don't really mind
You're so gentle and kind
And such a sweet little dog
And you do sleep like a log!
Wake up . . . walkies!

Theresa Hartley-Mace

When Harvey Met Jo

No! We are not getting
Another cat
And that is that
Not another cat . . .

Well, what was I supposed to do
When you looked at me with eyes of blue?
So intently, never averting your gaze
That said - you're going to love me all of my days

A furry scrap that cried when alone
If ever I dared from your side to roam.
So in my pocket you'd hitch a ride
Still to this day - always by my side.

How could I resist that bundle of joy?
That is now my big Harvey, my gigantic boy.
Who is big and broad and furry and strong
Yet still such a coward it seems so wrong!

But that is part of your enduring charm
My gentle giant with a heart so warm.
You give me so much affection and love
Truly a wonderful gift from above.

You make me laugh when I am down
Being such a clutz, such a clown.
I love the funny things you do each day
You knew you were always going to stay.

Joanna Malone

Ball Of Nuisance

I was just a young pup,
And you were getting on.
I knew we were a partnership,
Although not for very long.

Back then I pushed you and I pulled you,
And I tried to ride you round.
But you never did get angry,
In fact, you kept me safe and sound.

You guarded at the front door,
And you stood there by my chair.
I was this little ball of nuisance,
To which you gave your love and care.

And soon you were to leave me,
Just so you know, I grew up fine!
Sorry for being that ball of nuisance,
But I couldn't tell you at the time.

Geoff Ward

Jess

Morning mist shrouds the approach.
Silent strategy and snakelike slithers
separate the dewy blades.
A mission to maul in commando crawl
fuels her daily raids.

Priming of the lethal claw,
camouflaged by glossy paw
heralds avian death.
Feline reaper, Jess the Ripper
grim dispatcher of last breath.

Her collar bell knells for hearts condemned
that fall from downy chests;
signed and sharply slashed
with a flourish, in a signature J.
Her precision weapon aimed to punish
visiting flying prey.

A psychopathic primal urge
fires nature's cruel killing purge.
Smugly blameless, life-cycle factor
super-efficient culling contractor.
When the fluttering has cessated
Jess is never wholly sated.

There's no rest when there are nests,
furry vile eggs-terminator!

Anna Dimakopoulou

Independent Felix

Dear Mr Bigfoot - I've something to say
I'm sick of being treated
Like an animal each day
You talk in weird human words, I just don't understand!
You lift me up and toss me round
And pat me with your hand
Another thing - about my door, I'm sure that you'd agree
Headbutting is not something
That is civilised for me
And as for all your sofas - I don't think it's fair
That I can't sit on any one
In case I leave some hair
I'm an independent Felix, with a reputation to maintain
So I ask you politely - please
Don't embarrass me again.
Don't call me like a common cat, where everyone can see
I'll come to you on my own terms
I'm not your pet, I'm free
Don't make friends with the neighbour's cats I don't associate
With common riffraff full of fleas
You stroke them - big mistake!
And don't think Sir that the meat you give is the best I ever get
I've fifteen dinners on my round
Each house thinks I'm their cat
I've heard it said that I am cute -
Handsome, pretty - maybe sweet
So Sir, you're lucky I stay with you
Even if you've the best house on the street.

Sarah Clayton

When I Was Two

When I got you
I was only two
We were small and young
And you ran away when I sung
I love the way you used to purr
When I sat next to you and stroked your fur

You've been gone for a few months now
All I want is to hear you miaow
I hope you are safe and happy
And not looking old and shabby
Rest in peace my darling Rosie
Make yourself nice and cosy

One day we will be together
I hope you're not clawing any leather
This is my poem for you
I'm glad I got you when I was two.

Charlotte Julie Moffatt

Black Dog

Two alert brown eyes behind a long pointy snout
Four gangly legs, black and red flecked short-haired coat.

Got her from a dogs home in deepest dark Bath
Forlorn looking and shy made her hard not to have.

It seems that she'd certainly been put through the mill
As if she was shell-shocked she couldn't keep still.

Flinching and barking at the very least sound
In the beginning 'twas the way with our Sasha we found.

But now that she's older and wiser and stronger
Her scatty and neurotic ways are no longer.

With her pointy-ears and sure gait she proudly strolls round
Heckles quickly rising when she's standing her ground.

Getting that bit older she totters a little too
With her days left of stalking getting fewer and few.

Not as restless now, at least starting to slow down
And slowly lifting from her brow is her studious frown.

Although often looking these days worn-out, helpless and frail
Soon revives with a skip and flick of a long ropey tail.

Dignified and graceful in her prime as now she is known
Pleased that at the end that she found a good home.

Philip Graham King

My Dog Is Called Flap

His coat is brown and black
And when you take him out for a walk
Shout and he should come back.

All night he sleeps in his basket
Sometimes you can hear him snore
And when he is asleep
He can be quite a bore.

He is straight up in the morning
He is active and fit
Because he knows he is going for a walk
He is excited and he will not sit.

He chases all the birds
He is scared of cats and dogs
And when you throw a stone to him
He jumps up like a frog.

Nathan Waters

Last Of The Summer's Swine

With whiskers on the end of a nose that was long,
Eddie was a Jack Russell with a dash of Papillion.
Gentle as a lamb, with the softest caress,
But when the postman arrived he would puff out his chest.
Taking on the stature of a dog twice as large,
When he heard the ding-dong at the front door he'd charge.
Squirrels and rabbits, perhaps even cats . . .
I'll tear them to shreds as they land on the mat!

After the ritual of today's morning post,
Eddie sits by the fire, as his dad eats his toast.
This summer from snacking, the hound grew slightly plump,
People thought he was a girl with babies in his bump!
He'd walk round the park and suck in his belly,
Until he got back home, then slump before the telly.
So no breakfast today, only dinner for this dog,
He wanted to be svelte, not look like a hog!

Once weight was gained, it was hard to get rid,
Of that soft, floppy bit that hung like a bib.
He had tried callisthenics and even gymnastics,
Making a trampoline from his mum's knicker elastic.
Tied between a tree and the old garden shed,
Burning off the calories, from being overfed.
Exercising in this way would rid many pounds,
As he bounced way up high, fifteen feet from the ground.

Now he could pose, being no longer bigger,
The girls turned their heads at his slender new figure.
Even chasing the ball had become so much fun,
He shot round the field like a bullet from a gun!
The fat on his tummy not weighing him down,
Or dragging his midriff along on the ground.
Before he'd lost weight, he was always outrun,
Now he was beating the beagle from number twenty-one!

Back on the lead, heading home from the park,
The winter sun setting and time for the dark.
Gulping down water, he knew he should lap,
It was time for his tea, then a much needed nap.
Earning his feed he had beef for his dinner,

The food he had yearned, now that he was thinner.
Now falling asleep with legs that are twitching,
Are you chasing a rabbit, or is your ear itching?

We have watched you grow from a tiny pink pup,
Who sneakily drunk tea from my best china cup.
On arrival to us you were scared of the dark,
And hadn't yet managed to find your best bark.
Instead you would yelp and cry like in pain,
Especially when having to walk in the rain!
And so Eddie Jones, this poem I have penned,
For my greatest companion and best furry friend.

Michael Jones

Myfanwy

Myfanwy is her name
Our salt 'n' peppered Mini Schnauzer

And protection is her game
So 'next to nothing' will arouse her

She'll bark at strangers
And our friends
And seems to get the hump

But it's all for show
How do I know?
Her wagging little stump

She can make a noise
That is for sure
And for some she gives a fright

But I'm absolutely positive
She would never ever bite

She really likes most people
And hates it when they go
If I was Dr Dolittle
Her bark would say hello
Or can I have a carrot?

She wants to go out to the park
She loves it when out walking
Meeting other doggy pals
Always gets her talking

They come to sniff
She goes to ground
I wonder, why do that?
I sometimes think our little dog
Might be a scaredy cat

She came from Wales
Hence Myfanwy
Though now we call her Miffy
It could be that my lack of Welsh
Is why she's sometimes iffy

The language barrier is to blame
She runs and won't come back
So I guess she doesn't understand
That I'm the leader of the pack

(Humph . . . who am I kidding?)

Dave Baxter

Taca

A tiny bundle of black and white fluff
Yet still with unseeing eyes
So tiny and defenceless
That day you came into our lives

Many days and nights have passed by
Since that memorable day
And you've grown into a canny bitch
So fearless strong and brave

The rats and mice inhabiting
Our garden live in fear
And never venture out
When they know that you are near!

Butterflies and even frogs
Birds and snails and bees
All are at the mercy
Of your canine curiosity

Your agility is astounding
Never ceasing to amaze
Leaping, romping and delving
Obeying your instinctive ways

Let your questioning wet muzzle
Your unexploited heart
Your innocence and devotion
Remain with us till death us do part.

Susan Roberts

Kimba, The White Ninja

Fleet of paw and sharp of claw
Fangs so white but beware they bite
My tail is black and my fur is white
When I stalk by I'm quite a sight.

I purr and miaow with all my might
When I am loved or when I fight
My scars are from battles galore
When I win you'll hear me roar

My prey awaits in your back garden
Birds or mice and plenty of them
With stealth and cunning my aim is dinner
Am I really such a sinner?

My former owners abandoned me in a bin
My God I was so thin
I was rescued by the RSPCA
And I lived to fight another day

So now I do what comes naturally
For I am just a cat you see
My owners call me Kimba
But you had better call me the White Ninja.

Andrew Hudson

Watchers

If you know where to look, and turn your head nice and slow,
You'll spot a little cat watching to see where you go

They watch from the fences and up in the trees,
They sit in the windows and sniff at the breeze.

If they see you looking, they're just enjoying the sun,
Rolling on driveways and having some fun.

But as soon as you pass they make their report,
'My owner's gone shopping; I'll see what he's bought.'

Meeting on fences, in woods and on hutches for rabbits
The cats compare notes on their owner's strange habits.

'Mine pushes me out when I want to come in,'
'Mine makes me eat food that comes from a tin.'

'Mine buys me a mouse and invites me to play,
When I bring in a real one they whisk it away!'

'Mine lays out black clothing so I've somewhere to sit
Then gets all upset at the white fur on it!'

The cats yowl and miaow late into the night
Then return to their homes before it gets light.

All that they want is somewhere friendly and warm
A family to love them from the moment they're born.

To feed them on fishes to fill up their tummy
To fuzzle their bellies when the weather is sunny.

A cat in every home, an owner for each feline,
Their plan for the world is completely benign.

So, if you're lucky enough to have a cat in your home
To provide him a cushion and a cat flap to roam.

He'll report to the others that he's loved and well fed,
That this is an owner that gives up their bed.

And although he'll scratch at the sofa and sometimes go missing,
You'll be confused by his language, purring then hissing.

He might nip at your hand as you fuss under his chin
And yowl like a banshee if you won't let him in.

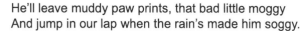

He'll leave muddy paw prints, that bad little moggy
And jump in our lap when the rain's made him soggy.

Head under your chin, all purring and rumbly
His fine fur will crackle as you rub at his tumbly.

And because you love him his bad ways are forgiven,
Even stealing away with pieces of chicken.

You'll smile and you'll laugh every time that you see him,
Tracking a bug that's up on the ceiling.

You'll love him for always and he'll love you back,
He'll always bring happiness that little loved cat.

This is why the cats watch - bad humans are rife,
But if you're a good one, well,
You'll be stuck with cats for the rest of your life!

David Bailey

Bonnie

(An English Setter sadly missed)

There are a crowd of daffodils growing on your grave,
And at its head a large grey granite stone
To mark the spot.
But I am sure had you the voice to speak
You wouldn't even want an ornamental pot.
Strong limbed and free you'd much prefer to be
Around my garden, playing in and through the shrubs,
And every step close following me.

Your leaping energetic movements,
Gaping, grinning mouth, and ears a flap
You would assuredly be investigating
Every moving blade of grass,
You'd need no map
To traverse swiftly the lengths of lawn,
My Bonnie girl, by nature bonny too.

You'd flop down panting at my feet
Tongue a loll, glistening with moisture
Like some diamond mine exposed to light
And eyes fixed lovingly to me
You'd pant in urgent beat

Until quite overcome, all energy spent
You'd lie muzzle along the length of paws
And close your eyes, and in an instant sleep
And time to time you'd gently mash your jaws.

Oh how I miss you Bonnie girl!
The emptiness that still assails my soul,
Even after all this time!
It never leaves, and takes its daily toll.
The daffodils remind me your earthly bones are there
But I am sure your essence roams more elysian fields
Than this bright garden here, that's mine.

And when you come to rest
You'll lay your silken head
Before the Being who created such as you,
A perfect poetry of motion, energy
And unconditional love

106

You may be gone from me
But I believe you are not dead.
I hear you panting still
And I hear your neat nails tap, tapping on the stairs above.

Teresa Wallace-Reynolds

He Sits Amid The Daisies

He sits amid the daisies
All silky black and purring
Ears twitching as he contemplates
The sparrow in the trees

Then stretching forth his graceful limbs
Resplendent tail unfurling
Yawns lazily, his silken coat
Stirs softly in the breeze

He sleeps beneath the hedgerow
All curled up and unstirring
Contented in his kingdom
Prestigious and wise

Then waking from his slumber
As if driven by a yearning
Prowls silently, the hunger
Burning in his emerald eyes

He plays among the crocuses
As autumn leaves are turning
Springing from the fence post
On his unsuspecting prey

Then whiskers twitching suddenly
Intuitive, discerning
Discards the game, the sparrow
Lives to fight another day.

Julie MacDonald

Sam Is A Bag Of Fun

The young pup comes rushing into the family room,
running at the sound of me playing the piano.
Floppy ears, rough black and white fur,
smiles with all his teeth,
less then ten pounds to him.
He slides a bit across the hardwood floor,
sits himself down on his rump and begins to howl.
Not a deep melancholy howl to his ancestors,
but a high-pitched puppy howl.
I stop playing. Maybe he doesn't like Mozart?
He looks at me, cocks his head to one side.
I hit some notes. Sam resumes howling.
I perform a simple scale. He does not follow,
he is not vain enough to howl in key.

In the wild wolves howl for many reasons:
upon waking, after play or social interactions,
bonding among pack members, because they enjoy it.
Wolves love to howl. Barry Lopez observed:
'I've even seen a wolf in air of not wanting to miss out,
howl while defecating.'

Having spent many a season chained
to the mirror and the razor blade.
A slave to the black dog. Now, sober,
sane, no stranger to death.
Sam now. Sam might be on to something.
Fitting in, having fun, being a part of,
howling, the voice of a social jest.
I get down from the piano bench, on all fours
Sam watches me closely.
I start to howl. A broken, delighted sound.
Sam looks startled, but soon joins in.
I have made a new friend.
Sam is a bag of fun.

Philip Shackleton

A Promise

I heard today that many cats who look a lot like you,
Are being thrown out on the street (along with doggies too).

The credit crunch is blamed for this; I've seen it on the news,
Jobs are really hard to find, and easier to lose.

Some people who can't keep their pets, they do the proper thing,
They ask the kindly shelter folk if they will take them in.

But others do not seem to care and simply let pets go
To wander, lost, alone and scared, through ice and rain and snow.

When I first brought you home with me, two tiny balls of fluff,
I swore that I'd take care of you, even if life got rough.

Now money's right and times are hard but still you're here with me,
I'd sell my soul to keep you fed and warm, as cats should be.

Now you're not perfect, that's the truth, you do some silly things,
You jump and hiss at the telephone, every time it rings.

You disappear for hours on end; I panic about the road,
Then in you'll stroll quite casually, with a bird or a mouse (or a toad).

You demand cuddles constantly; you think you own my lap,
You'll chase each other in and out and smash through the cat flap.

Some people say you're lucky cats, to have an owner like me,
Someone who feeds and cares for you, yet still lets you be free.

But I think I'm the lucky one, and here's the reason why,
You purr and play and make me smile, even when I cry.

I wish that I could help more cats and keep them here with you,
For now a few pennies to charity, is all that I can do.

However, you two are my own,
and have been from the start,
When you both curled up in my lap
and claimed my barren heart.

So every day I say these words,
through poverty, fear and strife,
I'll keep you safe, my lovely cats;
you have a home for life.

Victoria Walklate

My Budgie

My budgie quite likes a good rhyme
But he's old now and well past his prime
He used to be cute
Now he's just deaf and mute
So I do him some couplets in mime.

Geoff Lowe

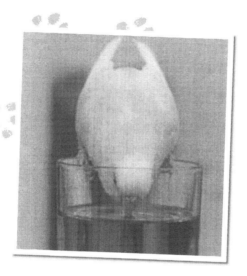

Animal Antics

Cats prowl, scaring,
For, glaring out
They are seen
In the dark.

Cats are actors
Appearing as
Pantomime's
Puss in Boots.

Cats play with balls
Amusingly,
With two paws
They will pounce.

Cats spring up high,
Limbs extended
They're adept
And balanced.

Cats take pleasure
In sunbathing,
Stretched out,
Lazily.

Cats are alert
To weather change,
Behaving
Quite strangely.

Cats sense alarm
If music notes
Frequently
Are high-pitched.

Cats are intrigued
By cars when parked,
Having sense,
They adapt.

Cats advertise
Convenient
Tasty snacks
'Like nibbles'.

Cats are admired
For their beauty,
White coated
Most of all.

Cats, logical,
Fond of number
Are thought to live
Some nice lives.

Christine Vaughan

Confession

I have a secret lover
She is so sweet and kind
I cannot help but love her
She's scarcely out of mind.

We meet up every morning
And afternoon and night,
Sometimes down the garden path,
Where I hold her tight.

If I hold her close to me
And try to pull away,
She grabs me with both her arms
And pleads with me to stay.

I know she is in love with me
Although she has not said,
But if I allowed her to
She'd follow me to bed!

I've really loved her all her life
And will do to the end.
I'd better come clean right now
She's Sylvia, our cat and friend.

She brings me meaty presents
She's surely in a flummox
She thinks the way to all men's hearts
Are through their bloodstained stomachs.

James Proudlove

Unusual Places

Theatre's glow,
With advertisement lights.
Stop and go
Of traffic lights.

Mighty roar of city traffic,
Carbon emission is terrific,
In most unusual places
Thriving city wild life is base.

Little mouse
Devoted little chap
Drags his dead spouse
Through a tiny gap.

Feral pigeons
With deformed feet
Feed on thrown away bread
Instead of wheat.

Sly trot
Of urban foxes
Hunting their ancient spots
Amongst thrown away supermarket boxes.

On tops of roofs
Starlings roost
Drawn by few degrees extra heat
Ever watching for anything to eat.

The lovely urban collared dove
City's symbol
Of peace
And love.

Bryan Clarke

Hairy Dog

Hairy Dog loves to play
and run around outside.
Disappear down a rabbit hole
what's down there inside?

Hairy Dog spies the bin
wants to have a look.
Head right over, topples in
landing in the muck.

Hairy Dog, soggy dog
rolling in a puddle.
Silly Billy, chilly dog
now he needs a cuddle.

Hairy Dog in a mess
matty, tatty, sore.
Itchy hot, chop the lot
Hairy Dog no more.

Fuzzy dog nice and clean
Trimmed and washed and dried.
Digging in the compost heap
still Hairy Dog inside.

Cav O'Neil

Marmalade

We have a family pet called Marmalade,
Our love for him will never fade.
He sleeps up on Grace's bed
And sometimes that is where he's fed.

Grace is ill and has to stay in bed
Because of ME and a pain in her head.
Marmalade is such good company for her
Grace is so quiet she often hears him purr.

Although the curtains are always closed
Marmalade creates a certain pose
Then jumps up on the window sill
To eye up birds while Grace takes her pill.

Marmalade is the ideal pet and
Grace's eyes are always set
On his orange eyes, soft clean fur
And his gentle soothing purr.

Marian Lang

Charley

She lay within a box
Among her sisters coated stripes
She was the odd one out
In her fur of black and white

She raised her gaze towards me
With eyes of brightest green
She truly without doubt
Was the cutest cat I'd seen

Without a moment's hesitation
I knew she was for me
So odd in tangled stripes
I wanted to set her free

So I paid the Cats Protection
And our journey was begun
Homeward-bound we travelled
Then started all the fun

She keenly did explore
All that was strange and new
Curtains were Mount Everest
Shoelace tails worthy to chew

By night she was asleep
Snuggled cosy in my bed
The softest fur of black and white
Brushing gently against my head

In the morning I woke up startled
To find she was not there
I searched but could not find her
My fear turned to despair.

Then came the softest whimper
From the drawer below my bed
I opened to see piercing green
Peeping warily ahead

My fear dissolved that moment
And I laughed at such a sight
Tangled up in jumpers
Was her fur of black and white

I knew that very instant
We would never be apart
Felt her little pawprint
Etched forever in my heart

Five years on she now has grown
Although she's still the same
A cat saved form a cardboard box
Charely is her name.

Amanda McLellan

It's A Cat's Life

The sun's coming up
I open my green eyes
I scan the room around me
Another day in paradise

I meander over
To where my food bowl lies
Whiskas finest duck
My delight I cannot hide

I deserve a rest
From a hard morning's work
My housemates want to fuss me
In a minute I'll go berserk

There's a time and a place
For attention and play
Right now I want to sleep
I'm the boss, so do as I say

They need to be kept in check
These needy housemates of mine
They disturb me while I sleep
Too often of the time

So off now I'll go to sleep
The sun is still too high
I'll bide my time just perfectly
I'll wait until it's night

Several hours pass
And I'm ready for the hunt
A mouse or a bird, I don't mind
And I'll leave them all out front.

Sarah Doffman

Felix

Felix when I first saw you
A little kitten
You were the one for me
The loveliest I could see
You were so happy to be with me
And you liked your own territory
A large garden open and free
Grass to roll in you see
And trees to climb for you and me
You were young and full of fun
Later on you settled down
But still liked to play around
You were very quiet and sweet
So in bed you liked to lie at my feet
Then you had your first litter
Then another but all kittens were put away
But with your third, one would stay
This other was a lovely kitten
This was Darkie, black and white
Soon to be part of our life
Felix went to get an operation at the vet
When he did this he saw a large tumour
He told my father she had not got long
One day I found her lying by a tree
She had come to die beside me
My love for her is still with me.

Gordon Forbes

My Wiggly Giggly Cat

My cat is a wiggly giggly sort of cat
Who makes me laugh
When I wear him around my neck
Like an expensive cashmere scarf.
He sleeps where he wants to
Usually in my bed
Like a big Russian hat on top of my head.
He eats toast for breakfast
And fish fingers for tea
Secretly supplied under the table by me.
He rolls on his back
Showing his tummy
So I tickle him, his tricks are so funny.
He rattles his cat flap
And wakes me at night
So I know he's safe after another cat fight.
But he's got a dark side
That's not very nice
As I've witnessed his ability to stalk and kill mice.
He came as a kitten
A gift quite free
But my beautiful cat is now priceless to me.

Owen Gourdon

Pauline And Friends Card Making Blog

Twiglet glares his 'Heathcliffe' stare,
Moody and troubled
He's a handful, there's no doubt,
But Pauline wouldn't be without her feline friend,
Though he has been known to drive her 'around the bend'.
Scattering debris,
Scraps of glitter and ribbons,
Stalking 'Whatnots' and buttons
Shuns 'Hugely Huggly' forums:
Sweet is not what he's about!

Endlessly inquisitive,
His careful observation
Scrutinises processes
Of greeting card creation.
He vows to evade such excruciating fates
As 'cropping' and 'snipping' or
Getting squished by the 'Sizzix',
Though a bit of glue sniffing does not go amiss -
Years of misuse mean catnip
Ceases, now, to stimulate!

Hearing his mistress complain
Of days, she feels, are 'wasted',
Twiglet sneers disdainfully
At, he feels, distress misplaced.
He still bears a grudge, recalling last year's trauma,
When, in a fudge-fuelled frenzy,
She, 'widened her horizons'. Prancing off to France!
Pauline ignoring his frantic caterwauling,
Unaware it could be traced
To inside her own suitcase!

Ella Lloyd

Molly

The RSPCA - they seem so nice - but they've a lot to answer for,
Those pleading, soppy adverts that get you through the door.
A dog to walk and cuddle, a pet who needs a home,
Why not? We thought naively, and got straight on the phone.
An older dog would suit us; six or seven would be great,
And so they showed us Molly, who was about one hundred and eight!
She plodded into the room, a dopey senile fool,
She rubbed her ears across my knee and smothered me in drool.
She had the floppy ears and the tilted silky head,
'Nobody else would want her, she's far too old,' we said.
And so we did the honours, we signed on the dotted line,
We set off to collect her thinking things will be just fine.
They're really rather sneaky though, that RSPCA.
They let us fall in love with her before they chose to say,
'Oh yes, she has a few small lumps, they shouldn't do her harm,
Did we mention that she's deaf as well; it's all part of her charm.
Her teeth are rotting slowly and her legs aren't what they were,
And you might want to fix these bundled knots that are breeding in her fur!'
Okay, so we're up for a challenge, and that was what we had.
It was time to lose any sense of pride in our newly married pad!
First there was the issue with closing any doors,
The crazy eyes, the panting and the frantic pacing paws.
Then three o'clock each morning, the desperate toilet dash,
Leap out of bed and down the stairs before we heard a splash!
The overdraft was useful when arthritis then set in,
The vets smiled sweetly as they asked - another seraquin?
Feeding chicken from my hand, carrying you to the lawn,
Mopping twelve o'clock at night and then again at dawn!
Poor Molly, we sometimes wonder how we coped, I don't know how,
But I know I'd mop a million floors to have one cuddle now.

Debbie Hollingdrake-White

Walkabout Puppy

Now that I am bigger there are big dog things I do,
I wait until I am outside to do my puppy poo.
When we're going for a walk and come up to a tree,
I proudly cock my leg instead of crouching for a pee.

The bestest thing I love is when I'm able to run free,
And this is cos I've learnt to come back when I'm called you see.
I sniff at other doggie's bums and want them to play too,
But if they bark, I'll only peer at them from behind you.

My nose is to the ground and I just love to have a snoop,
It really makes me happy when I'm sniffing doggie poop.
I hear you say 'that's nasty' and pull me away real quick,
When I eat drunkard's hamburgers and then lap up their sick.

We always go out for a walk come wind or rain or shine,
I zigzag on the pavement, never walk in a straight line.
We finally get home again, the end is bitter sweet,
I always get a cuddle and a very tasty treat.

Yvonne Nowakowski

Our Miniature Poodle

Why do we love thee, Poppy our dear,
Since you sulk and growl at us all without fear.
You tell us all off if we sit on your chair,
But when food is about you stand there and stare.
Unlike other poodles, you eat all kinds of food,
Lettuce, cucumber and even horse poo!
You are old and moody but your love we all share;
Without you, Poppy, our cupboard would be bare.

Eda Hughes

A Pussy Cat's Plea (From Beyond)

My empty void you must surely fill
Don't put up brick walls around your heart
Because you feel torn apart
Please let another little cat into your life.

Don't grieve so much, that you feel ill
I'm not so far away,
I know that you love me, and I love you still
It won't be the same but you've got nothing to lose, only to gain.

Although sometimes you may feel
As though you've had enough of life
And all of its bitter pills
A different bond will form in time
And you will love again.

Think of me often, tuck me into a corner of your heart
And shelter me there from all of your tears, as though from rain
I know new love will ease your pain.

And, I will wait, until the end of time,
To be held in your arms once again.
I'll be there for you at Heaven's gate
Your ever-loving friend and your best mate.

NJ Brocks

Forest Trails

No more can I run out into a garden
And we are far from the countryside.
It's been ages since my last truant
On a third floor, we now reside.

Aditya lives in a different city
The house-help has chores to attend.
Nikki walks me only reluctantly
My walks are thus brief events.

It's unlike my life in Nainital
Walks with Aditya were in fact, hikes.
The great outdoors was a shared passion
Irresistible was the countryside.

The Nainital we know lies undisturbed
Of cliffs, streams and forest trails,
Tucked away in a corner of the Ayarpatta
Where nature still reigns.

I was spared the leash on these outings
And a model behaviour I displayed.
Amidst the rhododendron, oak and ash trees,
My wanderlust was tamed.

Horses were respectfully given way
And I didn't claim a territory for too long.
I was cordial to the occasional passer-by
Birds weren't game; I was game for their songs.

I recall spotting barking deer
And losing them, moments into the chase.
But Aditya ensured he never lost my trail
By his side, I was safe.

Unfulfilled is the wanderlust
I want to prance on those familiar trails
Even if it's on three faltering limbs
Despite the struggle and the fall from grace.

Aditya N S Nabial

Moose

We have a dog called Sam
And all he does is bark
In the house,
Down the caravan
Even on the park.

Samson is his full name
And occasionally he whistles
When he sees a dog
Or even a cat
Also on the field among the thistles.

Now Sam is his name
But I call him Moose
It came about
After a time
We didn't want to let him loose.

Jonathan Simms

DeeZee Dog

Her name is DeeZee
She was a freebie
From a lad going overseas
He needed a home
Where she wasn't alone
With her toys and bone
So she soon settled in
Our pet number seven
And mini whirlwind
As she chases her tail
And woo woos and wails
And plays - she never fails
A Staffie cross-breed
Pointed lugs on her head
From an English Bull T?
She gives us a laugh
Is quite clever by far
And very much a character
We have loved all our pets
From each one we've met
There is not a bestest yet
It's not fair to say
To judge or grade
As differences never fade
DZ our friend
Will be loved till the end
Before she goes to Heaven
And there she'll see
Murphy and Lucy
Shmoo and Sparky
Molly and Alfie
Who are already there
But for now alive and well
She's sleeping - you can tell
The house is far too still!
That she shares with two cats
Judy and Thor, doggie Staffs
And us, complete DZ's path
So far.

Diane Simpson

Bess The Boxer Cross

(This short poem is dedicated to my lovely Boxer cross Staffie bitch, Bessie, and to all those poor abandoned doggies in need of a loving home)

I bought our Bess when just a pup
And now four years of love gone by
She's at my side when I wake up
There when I laugh or cry
For there can be no better friend
Nor loyalty compete
Companion till the very end
Bess made my life complete

So should you see us in the park
Or walking in the countryside
Remember reading how it starts
And why I feel so warm inside
Do you have the time and place
And room within your heart
Go get a dog to share your space
And never ever part.

Ellis Williamson

Pawprints

When a person gets a dog
they know they'll love it so,
but never can anticipate
how that love will grow.

A dog will be your faithful friend
loyal, brave and true,
companion and protector
and always there for you.

Through the playful puppy days
chewing things and bouncy ways,
you'll look on them with fondness
and wish they wouldn't fade away.

As an adolescent dog
never tiring, chasing sticks
always walking by your side
or learning to perform new tricks.

Through the seasons, through the years
you'll watch your old dog grow,
eventually the time will come,
time to let him go.

Although it will be painful,
and many tears you'll cry,
he'll know how much you love him
when it's time to say goodbye.

The memories will stay with you
of years you spent together,
happy days of walks and play
will be with you forever.

When you decide to get a dog
be warned right from the start
although eventually he'll leave you,
he'll leave pawprints in your heart.

Sarah Barrie

Not A Bear, But An Aire . . .

'Is that a bear?' the little girl whispers,
peeping wide-eyed, from behind her mother.
'I don't think so,' says Mum, 'at least, probably not,
I don't think they have bears in Wiltshire.

He's certainly furry; you could almost say 'grizzly'
and those paws look perfect for scooping up fish,
but those paws don't have claws, well, not very big ones,
and I can't get a look at his teeth.'

'Not nearly a bear,' I laugh, 'but an Airedale.
I suppose I see how you might be mistaken.
A teddy bear, yes, as he's not very fierce,
though he likes to pretend with the postman.

He's desperately in need of a really good haircut,
so's looking a trifle more woolly than usual.
You should see him after, it's really quite funny,
he looks so much more like a weasel.

But he's no weasel, or even a bear, but an Airedale
with furry front legs and big bushy beard,
and a tail that curls like a Cumberland sausage,
and a mischievous mind full of Airedale ideas.

He'll lie on our bed, just to say that he's been there,
and chases the squirrels, which just makes them laugh,
and gives you 'that look' when called to come in,
that says, 'I think not, I'm busy, thanks very much.'

But he loves nothing more than a scratch and a cuddle
and sleeps like a sentry at the top of the stair,
and welcomes us home with such joy and excitement.
He's a funny old stick, not a bear, just an Aire.'

Kate Clark

The Prowl

Soft, padded paws upon the ground
And twigs beneath her feet.
The cracking echoes stir around
The cat - the killer - leaps.

The forest mirrors fur of black
And hides her tracks with night.
The darkness like a velvet cloak
Wherein her prey takes flight.

Now stones beneath her feet seem hard
At dawn she travels home.
From now until tomorrow's dusk
She'll watch the world alone.

Frances Moldaschl

Unconditional Love

Unconditional love
I give,
Although,
He's snooty
He's arrogant
He's greedy
He's fickle
If you haven't got food he doesn't care
With his tail in the air he stalks away
His love is shallow
As his bowl
And yet
I quest for his love
Or acknowledgement
At least
He begs
He lies
He steals
But I love him,
For all that
He is my cat.

Katie Gisborne

Sheba (Doberman)

She came to us all legs and soft brown almond eyes
She took over our home and our hearts
And our lives were changed from that day on.

Her puppy mischief made us laugh
As she would give us cause to laugh throughout her life.

She was mother to our children and smaller animals, protecting, guarding
and ever gentle.
Unconditionally she gave to us her love, loyalty and faithfulness.

She loved to play and romp and run forgetting to be sedate and noble as
befits her breed
But she thought it silly to go walking in the rain.

We do not really need the little carved stone beneath the apple tree to
remind us
She is ever in our hearts and minds, in our memories and reminiscences.

My lovely Sheba! Maybe one day there may be another dog to fill the empty
void
But not yet, no, not yet.

Ann Dempsey

Reflection Of Jandaw Big Ben, Boxer Boy

A man is sweeping winter leaves away
Red rusty coloured leaves familiar as the skies
Reminds me of your red coat, your pansy black eyes.
A reflection.

Now a big paw greeting me as I descend the stairs,
A cold nose snuggling into my affection,
A welcome back even when I only put the rubbish out for collection.
Five years to the day I bid goodbye to my old Ben.
He was a figure of perfection.
Strange but nice to have you here
A look-a-like selection.
Your shiny red coat, your smooth pansy black eyes,
Ben's reflection.

Maxine Jackson

Running Into Trouble

Guard
'Case number 127 your honour!'

Judge
'Thank you, Hamster rise, you are convicted of crime.'

Hamster
'Judge, tell me of my crime?
I will clear it in rhyme.'

Judge
'Son, you are wanted for running,
Running too fast on your wheel.
I understand you think you're cunning
You're way too loud the humans feel.
How do you plead?'

Hamster
'Not guilty!
Not guilty!

You see there is a simple reason why us hamsters run
It ain't for our enjoyment
It isn't any fun
It isn't to burn weight off
So I can strut my thing
It isn't to upset the humans
If that was the aim I'd sing.

But there is just one reason
Why us hamsters run,
It's for the twenty-six miles
Of the hamster marathon!'

Guard
'Judge says.

Judge
'Hamster, I'm not sure about your story
Let me hand you to the jury.'

Guard
'Jury say what you predict
Please stand up and give your verdict!'

Hamster
'I'm scared
Be prepared
No more running
I feel like a clown
No more marathon
Am I going down?'

Jury
'Not guilty!'

Hamster
'Hooray!'

Judge
'Son, the jury's decision has been made
You're one lucky pet
You're free, be gone with you
Your running days aren't over yet.'

Hamster - To the humans -
'On behalf of hamsters everywhere
From deserts to mountains white
We apologise for annoying you
And keeping you up at night

But there is just one reason
Why us hamsters run
It's for the twenty-six miles
Of the hamster marathon!'

Verity Huntley

Kitty Comes Clean

In my sandpit I once found
A smelly, somewhat squidgy mound.
I gingerly poked it with my finger
And found the stench did on it linger.
When I'd burnt it, Kitty said,
'I'll just replace it when I'm fed.'

So I asked her what it was,
That smelly, squidgy mound, because
In the sandpit, I'd just seen
Her pawprints where her mound had been.
When I told her, Kitty frowned,
And sheepishly stared at the ground.

'I think it's time that I come clean,
I find your cooking quite obscene.
I didn't want to tell you, though,
For the truth would hurt you so.'
My eyes watered, round with shock,
'You didn't like my cabbage wok?'

Kitty shook her head and sighed,
'Sorry, even then I lied.
I never even swallowed it,
But spat it out, on the sandpit.'
So I dug and found down deep
Many more a smelly heap.

Ever since that sorry day
Kitty cooks, to my dismay.

Anna Carlson & Karin Carlson

Tubby

'Can I rub my face on this?
Ooh, can I eat that?'
Surely these are the thoughts
Of my pot-bellied cat.

An odd patch of fur
Black marks on her head
Tubbs can usually be found
Curled up on my bed

Or else underneath it
Snoring away
Completing her feline 'to do' list
(The errands of the day.)

A routine of stretchin'
Snoozin' and lickin'
Barrelling through the door
Whenever Dad shouts, 'Chicken!'

Then she's back on my sill
Eagerly watching the birds
Swooping for bread
Among the grass and the firs.

Scratching the carpet
And ripping the sofa
Mom huffs and puffs
(But secretly loves her)

You've never met a cat
Who's quite as funny
As lazy, fluffy
Mischievous Tubby.

Georgina Lea

Tommy

Tommy is my neighbour's cat, in fact, he's one of three
The others, they don't visit, but Tommy's 'adopted' me
Each day he comes a-calling, he's there outside my door
He rushes in to greet me then rolls around the floor.

Tommy is a tabby cat of white and grey and brown
With big amber-coloured eyes that seem to look me up and down
He has a lovely nature, is affectionate and funny
He really hates the wind and rain, he much prefers it sunny.

Now Tommy likes to slope upstairs for a sleep upon my bed
A nice warm cosy duvet and a pillow for his head
Sometimes he likes to sleep outstretched, sometimes he's in a ball
But on his back with legs akimbo is the funniest of all.

Tommy loves a cuddle so he's soon up on my lap
He snuggles down then turns around and has a little nap
He likes a tickle on his head and underneath his chin
This produces lots of purring, it's really quite a din.

Tommy walks with a bit of a waddle, well, he is a little stout
The fastest I have seen him move is when there's food about
He doesn't show an interest in catching bird or mouse
But sometimes he has a manic spell and runs around the house.

Now Tommy, he's not stupid, he's quite a canny cat
He knows he doesn't live here; it's just a place he's at
But he brings a little sunshine to an ordinary day
I'm glad I've been 'adopted', so pleased he came my way.

Carolyn Jones

In Memory Of Rosie

The place feels so empty without you there,
The field just seems to be so bare.
But when I think of your cute little face and frizzy hair,
I remember all the good times that we shared.

You liked to keep Dave and Cobweb in their place,
Which often resorted to a nip on their face.
You were a tough little cookie that could put up a fight
This made up for your small but very neat height.

As far as you were concerned, nothing was allowed to be shared,
Poor Cobweb and Dave, but you didn't care.
Sharing at cuddle time was definitely not allowed,
As I found out so, when you gave me a bite on the leg and it began to
pound.

You would stand for hours,
As I groomed you from top to tail
Whilst you ate your way through a nice fresh bale.

I really loved working and jumping with you,
Especially when your confidence grew.
And when we spent time practising Parelli,
Even if it did mean you stood on my welly.

I was so proud of you at the riding club
When you won reserve champ in most appealing,
And you got excited and cantered around with your coat gleaming.

You were a special one of a kind Rose
And they are very hard to find.
But you will always have a special place
With your memories bringing a smile to our face.

Laura Nemeth

Freddy The Goldfish

Oh what gladness you do bring
And how you make my heart sing
Swimming round in a bowl
You bring more joy than you know
A free spirit that is you
Just a goldfish but I love you.

Lyn Hudson

My Dog Georgie

My day would mean little without him
His bark makes the sweetest sound
He is the funniest dog in the whole wide world
And he spins my head around
If the floor is too cold for his four paws
Then he will walk on just the front two
He is impossible to hide from
And his face says, 'Hey look, I've found you!'
When his bowl is empty of water
He will always let me know
By picking it up in his sharp little teeth
And giving it an almighty throw
And when I'm curled up watching TV
And he knows I'm not ready to play
He will jump on the back of the sofa
And cover the leather in clay
But not all of his antics are crazy
He can be quite calm and serene
That is until he sees a football
And thinks that he's part of the team
But he's my little dog and I love him
With all of my heart and that's true
You sweet little Yorkie
You are loved more than words
My life would be dull without you.

C Dobbing

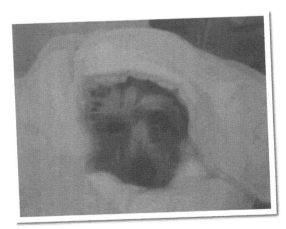

A Match Made In Heaven

I met this girl with big dark eyes
A beauty so deep it reflected my surprise
Her glossy hair sparkled in the light
A blissful black and a blonde so bright.

She looked up at me through the cold metal wire
Sun glittering in the distance like brilliant red fire
A deep wave of longing seeped into my heart
I knew there and then I'd not let us part.

She was just sitting there all alone
Sad and lonely, with nowhere to call home
I knew I must help her escape from this place
And bring back some joy to her beautiful face.

The keeper opened the big padlocked gate
Surely this match must be heavenly fate
Slowly she stepped out into the yard
Wearily looking up at the guard.

Her eyes pleading me not to turn from her light
Leaving her crying out into the night
I stepped towards her with a tingle down my spine
I want her, I need her, this girl will be mine!

Now whenever I walk into my house there's a whirl
And I'm greeted spectacularly by my gorgeous girl
Her tail wagging, her ears going floppy
My darling, my dog, my wonderful Poppy!

Sophie Scales

Donna Nobis

Donna nobis enters in, the babies' den
Blessed babies one short of ten
Plate in hand with Weetabix
She ventures into the battle mix
A well of puppies, in sleep blessed bundles of smooth soft pacifisms
Awake, gladiatorial full play with growls and snarls, bites and howls
Ineffectually puppyish
Mother comes authority, then single-minded suckles transcend
As if apotheosised from a lesser field
Ruthless juggling interceding, all laws of decorum left behind in heaven and position won
Won regardless of courtesy, deference or ranking, even size is not enough
Every little gap or opportunity is ruthlessly purloined.
Then suddenly blessed again in surfeit sleep nine mingled as one soft fur pudding limbs akimbo,
Stretching spider-like from a many legged puppy ball
It's animal carpet wall to wall.

Ernest Roberts

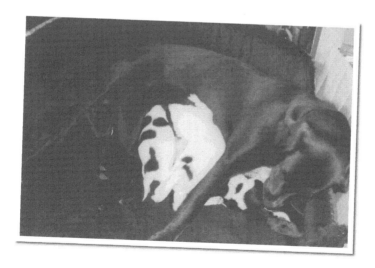

Untitled

Where have you gone?
You made me feel strong
I can't hear your paws
And you're not coming through any of the doors
You're not on my bed
Up close to my head
I know I used to shout
And tell you to get out
But I really do miss you
I wish you were here feeling like new
I took you out for a walk
And you were there when I needed to talk
You helped me when things got bad
And hugged me when I was upset with my dad
Brandy you were there for me
I just wish I was too
I miss my cuddles lying on you till I was asleep
You were more than a dog, you were my peep.

Sheryl Wood

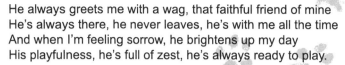

Rupert

He always greets me with a wag, that faithful friend of mine
He's always there, he never leaves, he's with me all the time
And when I'm feeling sorrow, he brightens up my day
His playfulness, he's full of zest, he's always ready to play.

I wander to the sitting room and slump into a chair
He comes and sits beside me, we really are a pair
His golden coat, his big brown eyes say look I'm here for you
He really loves me of that I'm sure; he loves me through and through.

We go for walks together, he rushes out the door
His eagerness for exercise I cannot but adore
And as we walk along the road, he sniffs and sniffs away
We reach the park; I let him loose, the highlight of his day.

He finds the biggest puddle, all muddy and brown
He jumps in it and splashes, he really is a clown
He looks up at me, his face all coy, with black marks in his fur
Hoping that his actions are okay and that I will concur.

At home again his playtime done a bath is what he needs
But getting clean is not his dream; he looks at me and pleads
A loving pat upon his head and into the bath he goes
He must endure, it's for his good, of that I'm sure he knows.

And then it's time for quiet again, we snuggle up together
We do this come rain or shine, no matter what the weather
He looks after me; he'll always be my crutch, my life support
I love him; yes I love him, my faithful friend Rupert.

Barbara Lambie

Bliss

She was once a kitten
A little bundle of fur
The first thing she learned
To do was how to purr.
She used to be quite sprightly
And would often jump
On top of the garden wall.
She could have scaled the trees
It didn't matter how tall
Showing no signs of fear at all.
But now the years have taken their toll
She is no longer a young cat
She is now very old
And with her advanced years
She no longer is so bold.
No more her games does she wish to play
Instead she wants to lay and sleep all day.
At twenty-seven she is past the pension
Age I have been told.
Her coat, which once was
Quite silky, has now lost its shine
Its gone quite tatty with the passing of time.
Her eyes they have gone dim
And sometimes she lies so still
It seems that there is no
Life left within.

Pauline Upichard

Ode To Rusty

A gentle walk in early June
through woods, so calm and shady,
in the fading light I saw your plight
and rescued you my baby.

Your leg was bound, wire wrapped round,
so tight on tiny limb.
Your body limp and eyes so wide
with thick lashes at the rim.

I took you home with Tess close by,
she loved you at first sight
and licked some life back into you
as you recovered from your fright.

You learnt to suck a drink of milk
and soon thought Tess was mum.
You hid away in meadow hay
but alas, your leg was numb.

Eight short weeks you lived with me,
so loving and so calm,
now I miss your squeak, your pattering feet
when I come home to the farm.

I miss the way you would suck my foot,
my knee, my toe or chin.
You really thought this was your home
and we were your next of kin.

The vet was sure we could do no more,
your little leg was cold,
so we said goodbye, poor little guy,
and I still cry.

You had a mum, I hope she knew I did my best for you,
but one thing's for sure,
the pain's still raw
and I couldn't have loved you more.

Caroline Knight

Paradise Ridge

(Dedicated to a black feral cat who knew she belonged to us, so sadly missed. Sweetie 1998/2005)

Paradise Ridge is a tranquil place, just before the other land
It's a stopping off place for cats and dogs of every kind, when they die.

Paradise Ridge repairs all cat and dogs to how we remember them, however they arrive
Before allowing them to wander, freely in the warmth and sunshine
Of the woods, meadows and fields.
There's water and their favoured food, and they tumble, frolic and play
As only cats and dogs can, no place for any animosity, they are all best friends.
Though their every need is taken care of, the lack of their owner's love is evident.
Paradise Ridge has a 'look out' and the view goes forever,
It's always warm and sunny there, and at least once a day all the animals will visit that spot.
Their visit is usually only a short one
They look far into the distance for the owners that they once dearly loved,
Be it yesterday or years gone by, the passing of time means nothing to them, as time stands still,
Their patience stands the test of time and they wait, unquestioningly.

Now and then one animal stands alone from the rest at the look out
They wait as only our loyal friends can
Each and every one of them, will, one day tread the same path.

We all pass Paradise Ridge on our way to the other land
Our four legged friends pick us out from afar
on our long journey, and they wait.

As we pass that point our loving
friends join us once again,
We look into their eyes and feel their warmth.
Together again with our loyal friends we travel
to the other land that seems so far away
Knowing that this time it's forever.

Norman Ian Armfield

Ever-Ready

Ever-Ready, should have been your name
Whether day or night, warm sun or rain
In darkness or in light, you are ready for the game.
Now dead to the world in deepest slumber and so far under
The Sandman's spell, it's hard to tell if you can move at all.
But not at all, no, none of that, for
The minute that I grab my hat, and gloves or shoes
What do you do? Every time, what do you do?

You jump and spring, wide-eyed, alert
As if to say, 'Hey, I'm ready, I'm ready, let's go!
I want to run and play and chase in the snow!'
You pirouette and woof, then run to the door
And lie in front of it so I can't ignore
The golden furred barricade, the immovable mass
Like ancient black magic that will not let me pass
Unless I speak word or do action akin to 'Open Sesame'

So I say, 'Come on then,' or simply grab the lead
And low and behold, it's a miracle see, the oceans have parted.
The path is free and I have a faithful companion to drag me along.
Because if it wasn't for you I wouldn't go out at all
On a day like today when it's cold and it's dark.
Yet once I'm out I grudgingly come round and enjoy it too
Because your zest is infectious and the sky is now blue.
And I'm glad you're ever-ready as I'm rarely anything but
So we make a great team me and my ever-ready, every-steady mutt!

Gerrard Moore

With A Wag Of His Tail

With a wag of his tail, he bounds to the door
His eyes seem to smile as he lifts up a paw
I open the door just a tiny wee crack
With a wag of his tail, he welcomes me back.

With a spring in his step he runs through the park
Urging me on with an impatient bark
He sniffs at the ground, pauses and then . . .
With a wag of his tail, he sets off again!

With a contented yawn, he climbs into bed
To dream of walkies, games and of being fed
He curls into a ball and snuggles down tight
With a snore and a whistle, he's out like a light.

Just a bundle of fluff, that's my canine friend
Curious, excited and loyal to the end
In good times and bad, when the stars all grow pale
He'll always be there with a wag of his tail.

Emma Tofi

A Trip To The Vet's (Alfie's Eye-View)

Hop out the car, not far to wander
the vet now makes me start to ponder
what once was such a super life
is fast becoming trouble and strife.

Fear exchanged with shortened glances
here two days don't fancy your chances.
Discussion goes on unabated
the vet's the one who's always hated.

The vet examines each worried pet
some get so worried the floor gets wet!
A short ponder them comes the frown
the time has come to put you down!

A burst of life, a sudden discovery
there's still a chance of full recovery.
A quick dash home before they get me
more speed driver, it's time I had tea.

My legs may wobble, my heart may murmur,
but I like it here on terra firma.

Chris Griffin

Rascat

Ras - as imperious as a king,
Whose green eyes with age grow dim,
Whose body trembles with staccato purr,
Long and sleek with downy fur.

As playful as a kitten still,
As you pounce and try to kill
A toy mouse on a piece of string,
With mock ferocity you spring.

In your sleep you twitch,
And dream you're hunting prey.
Then you yawn and stretch
And wash the dream away.

At night I hear you prowl
As you creep upon the stair.
Then you let out a mighty yowl
Just to remind me that you're there!

Doreen Morfitt

God's Creatures

Animals are not just for Christmas
They need a life of love and care
Cuddles and affection for everyone to share.

Cute dogs and adorable cats
Goldfish in their bowls and furry little rats.
All give out love as if wanting to say
Not in words but in their own special way.

Little kittens having fun, hamsters enjoying their cage
Wheel run, goldfish swimming all around their mouths
Opening and shutting without a sound
Puppy eyes that plead let's go for a walk
A colourful parrot having a squawk.

Floppy-eared rabbits running by the garden shed
Tortoises hibernating in their winter bed
So hold your little treasures and be there for them every day
Appreciate their presence in every loving way.

All need caring hands to cherish forever like a precious jewel
And lead them through a world that can be ever so cruel.

Irene Burns

Winston Hemingway

Winston is the perfect pet
The perfect pet for me
A guinea pig so wonderful
And fit for royalty

Winston is not tame or tidy
Believe me when I say
He's dafter than a lima bean
And cute in every way

Winston is like Dumbo
With ears so big and pink
But they're an important part of him
Those ears will never shrink

Winston's fur is so unruly
And falls off everywhere
But I could never ever cut it
I love his crazy hair

Winston can do tricks as well
And stand on his back feet
He's like a tiny puppy
And all he sees he eats

Winston lets his fur be combed
He loves to have a wash
And have his white fur blow dried
To make him look so posh

Winston is the perfect pet
The perfect pet for me
A guinea pig so wonderful
And fit for royalty.

Katy Holt

Mr Joney

Fuzzy, furry that's my cat
A little podgy, that's a fact
Bulging, black, beady eyes
Stretched out on the rug, there he lies.

Black and white like piano keys
He's always blanketed with fleas
Never says no when it comes to food
He farts on me, now that's just rude!

He never bothers to chase a mouse
Instead he lounges around the house
To sum, he may seem a pet
But to me he is simply the best!

Naseema Khalique

Domino

Domino, when you were young
You loved to run
Through house and yard
It was such fun.

And when they came -
The little grey men
Your heart would race
To get at them.

You jumped and whined
You begged them play
And play they did
It near turned you grey.

They swung in the trees
And sat on the pergola
Tempting you to catch them
The little grey men.

They would eat the wild fruit
Rob from inside too
And throw down some scraps
For you to chew.

They could clamber about
Tails hanging down
Your bark ascending
As you left the ground.

You would race round the pool
Leap in to stay cool
Leave a trail of water
To your next dancing duel.

What fun they gave you
And the odd feast too
When an avo dropped down
And it was all for you.

Now you are old
And I am too
The vervet monkeys still come
Do they remember us too?

Frank Gadd

Leo

Leonora
She found a home to be cared for
Never purred, only a squeak
It was all she knew to speak
Loving and friendly
A fine nice quality
She'll be missed by her sisters Lynx and Buttons
But her memory lives on
Now the tabby is gone.

T S

A Dog's Life

A dog's life is a dog's life
No matter what breed
Or if he or she.

A dog's life is a dog's life
If it's black or white
It can still fight.

A dog's life is a dog's life
If it's big or if it's small
If it crawls
Or it if falls
They're all the same
They just are different breeds and inherit different names
A dog's life is a dog's life . . .

Parisse Charles

Sandy My Ginger Tom

This is Sandy, my ginger Tom, matching white bib and socks,
He has a coat of long straggly fur and a tail as big as a fox,
Always washing, he nibbles out the knots and burrs,
Then sick next day from swallowing all the lumps of fur.
He answers to 'Sandy' or 'Basil' and understands, 'No! Good boy' and
'treats'.
He's very clever and smart, a little cracker, that's my canny ginger cat.

He was the runt of the litter, still feeding today as if he has to share it with
others.
He tells me when it's breakfast and tea, regularly at seven-thirty and then
half-past three.
His voice can be pathetic, quiet, except when he's in a brawl,
Then you'd think that the Earth had opened up and his cry was the Devil's
own call.
He's very brave, the leader of the pack, that's my bold ginger cat.

Once he disappeared for three days, I called him again and again, but
nothing.
Then, one day while washing up, a movement caught my attention.
I looked and saw a little face in a neighbour's garage window, he was
locked inside.
'Yes, could I have my cat back please, you've got him in detention.'
He was trembling and frightened so I cuddled him, my scared ginger cat.

Another time I caught him in a carpet van paws on the steering wheel, 'Get
out!' I yelled.
They say curiosity killed the cat and I know that one day his luck will run out.
He's always hiding under cars and then runs out when he sees ours,
miaowing.
We go for walks, at the end of the road he stops and naps, he knows I'll be
back
He's complacent, sometimes lazy, but he's family, my content ginger cat.

Often attached to his tail his friends from the garden, he will bring indoors.
There's baby slugs, even spiders and worms wriggling on the floor.
I'm forever cleaning up after him, especially the leaves and the twigs and
the dirt.
He looks at me with loving eyes and sits on my lap, purring, how can I be
angry?
He's very cheeky, knows he can get away with it, my cunning ginger cat.

164

He's fourteen years old but some days as young as a kitten, mischievous
and fun.
Ted, a tabby sometimes comes round; he lives across the road at number
twenty-one.
They do get on or seem to until I stroke Ted then Sandy sees him off,
resentful.
Then later he creeps on my knee, I stroke him and he smiles and plucks
contentedly.
I love him and he loves me, he's my friend for life, my faithful ginger cat.

Ann Blomley

The Little Tiger

Stealthily picking her way cross the sill
Suddenly sitting and staring - so still.
Looks through the windowpane (net curtains too)
Keeping her beady eyes also on you.

Ears twitching, tentatively, missing no sound
Whiskers that feel the vibrations around.
Leaping up lightly to snap at a fly
Looking on idly to watch life go by.
Guarding her territory out in the street
Picking up scents with her nose and her feet.

A solitary traveller, she roams wild and free
Bringing back tasty treats for you and for me.
Eats her food daintily, twitching her paws
Then she will brush your leg, waiting for yours.

Sleeping a good many hours on the bed
Waking you early, by nudging your head.
Darts up the garden when something goes by
Climbs up the tree and then perches - so high.

Scampers around without such a care
Likes to make sure though, that you will be there.
The little grey tigress is purring for you
Hoping you'll stay with her all her life through.

Helen Sarfas

Karma Rose

She curls into a ball
Karma is her name
And when she stirs and stretches her legs
It's time to up and play
We have to go to the forest
No alleyway will do
We'll walk to the woods or down by the lake
And if she's really good we'll go by the sea
Because the beach is her favourite place to be
She's very energetic and happiest when running free
She gallops a pace, with leg and body all sinewy
She'll charge through water and has jumped through fire
Amazing, is our Karma
And what about chasing rabbits, squirrels and even voles
It is a wonderful game she plays
And it's all okay, for those being chased
Are far too quick and before she can catch them
They've dived down holes or sprinted up trees
Her helicopter tail whirls
And then we pause
She makes my heart open as I watch her close
Oh her mud-spattered nose
Tickles me
Her lolling pink tongue and her sparkly eyes
Denote she is ecstatically happy
She is Karma
And after
Drinking water and wolfing a repas
She sits quietly
Enigmatically
Awaiting some petting
And she gets her treasured loving stroke
Then we pause
Activity over
Her magic still kindles
As she curls into a ball
She is Karma

Alicia Rose

Untitled

This monster's on my doorstep
I think he's here to stay
I'm trying all my best
Just to scare him away.

This ugly monster is big
He turns out to be like a pig
His body is fat
He eats like a cat
He doesn't at all
Look like a rat.

He's got lots of hair
Just like a bear
You don't at all
See him that rare
And if you saw him
You'd have a scare.

He's got yellow beady eyes
He never ever cries
He's got a nose like a mouse
He's never lived in a house.

He don't have a wash
He don't have no dosh
He is very dirty
And tends to be flirty.

This monster wasn't feeling good
He had a bit of a chill
He couldn't stop shaking
I knew that he was ill.

His eyes were red and watery
His nose kept running too
His cheeks were pale blue
So he frightened me too.

I took him to the vet
His nose was dripping wet
I tried all my best
Just to change his vest.

I brought him from the vet
He was very good
I took him to the house
He was as quiet as a mouse.

Leah Rees

Gerty Bendy Feet

My hen Gerty has strange bendy feet
She uses them mainly to find tasty things to eat.
She shuffles them about
Pulling disgusting looking morsels out.
Kicking this way and that,
Having a really good hard scratch.
When walking she hobbles,
Especially over the cold stone cobbles.
But over snow,
Boy, she really can go!
You see her bendy feet means she can really sprint
And makes the most wonderful unrecognizable dint.
Gerty BF was rescued one day
When a kind lady overhead her say,
'Please help me, I'm so alone,'
She whittered an almost inaudible moan.
Her hen house was completely bare
But there she was just right there,
Sat patiently on a concrete floor
Staring aimlessly up at the door.
She was waiting for another chance
A new life, some straw and hopefully, a playful dance.
So we rescued her, right there and right then
This beautiful hen.
New feathers they came
And a wonderful new name.
Gerty Bendy Feet
Isn't that just neat?

Robert Bullock

Sisters

It was on that day
They came my way
Two sweet baby girls
With pink paws and bellies
And ears full of curls
Eyes as bright as buttons
And two tiny black noses
Little tails wagging
All the beauty of roses
That was seven years ago
And to this day they are
My most treasured possession
Each one a little star
The love they give me every day
You simply could not buy
Sometimes they even talk to me
Well, they really seem to try
They are so happy always
From 'walkies' to 'taste' time
I'll be forever grateful
That those girls are mine
Drying wet bellies
After the rain
I'd be happy to do
Again and again
Their cuddles I'd give
Anything for
My heart leaps to see them
Waiting by the door
Those sisters love each other
As much as I love them
And I sometimes count the hours
Until I'm home with them again
I adore them so much
I have done since the start
When those tiny pink pawprints
Walked into my heart.

Marie Greenhalgh

Kittens Rule

While collecting our little tabby from the cat sanctuary
(Queen Mischa as she's now known to the family)
A small bundle of black fluff seized her chance
Introducing herself with a playful dance
Impossible to resist her sense of fun
We left that day with two, not one.

With her regal air, Mischa takes her throne
While Millie leaps about her new found home.
Those early days, full of silent fights
Chasing tails and whatever was in their sights.
These days, kitties exchange occasional affectionate sniffs,
The odd box around the ears, even royals have tiffs!

Queen Mischa and Princess Millie have loud contented purrs,
Not to mention the loveliest softest of furs,
Always scrupulously clean, an impressive undertaking
Especially as neither would ever dream of bathing
Unless you count getting drenched in a storm
When stubbornness prevents coming in where it's warm.

With winks and stares, they understand I'm sure
I get a chirpy 'hello' as they stroll in the door.
And Mischa, the adventurer, brings gifts for me,
'Dead mice,' I say, 'I do not want to see!'
So instead she brings one still alive
On the step she presents it, glowing with pride.
While I scoop up little predator, mouse runs free
But Mishca's contented, she's done something for me.

Millie revels in our company, it seems,
In my arms like a baby, she'll drift into dreams.
They share our lives and they've stolen our hearts
Our kitchen floor's permanently blessed with kitty paw marks.

Catherine Howarth

Buster The Dog

So here he is Buster, coat brown and black
If you look at him he'll always look straight back
He'll stare with wonder right into your eyes
And sometimes look with curiosity; is there a treat or surprise?

Although he has four legs, that's two more than me
Somehow he still understands 'walk', 'talk' and 'sit'
He's a clever old boy who's now learned how to open doors
With either a push from his head or he'll pull the handle down with his paw.

At just two years old he's very well behaved
Never needing a lead when bigger dogs approach
He stands tall, proud and brave
When it's time to move on even if the interest's still there
He'll switch off and walk with me without a care.

When he's hungry his ears stand straight and he holds this look
Food's definitely on his mind, the look can't be mistook
After his feed he gives a knock and a nod of thanks
And if I have a free one I'll scratch his jaw with my hand.

Then sometimes he'll do a strange 360° turn
And lay by the fire, sometimes I worry he may burn
But after a few minutes as the wise dog he is
He'll move a little further away on the red rug that is his.

This dear friend who's always been loyal to me
Helps me forget the strains and stresses that life can bring
And when I was told about the poetry competition, I thought I'd give it a shot
Because I know a pet who should win, it's Buster the dog.

Rupert Davies

A Story
(Dedicated to Wispa)

I climb the stairs and say goodnight
Jump into bed, turn off the light,
But I've forgotten every night
That someone has a story.
And it is sure I'll get no rest
For someone's going to be a pest,
Till I get up and do my best
To tell someone a story.
For that someone's climbed on the bed
Then grabs my arm and taps my head
Reminding me of things I said
That I'd tell them a story.
It's certain I will get no sleep
Till out of my warm bed I creep
And to someone my promise keep
By telling them a story.
I'll get no peace it's plain to see
For how persistent she can be
As she keeps on a-calling me
To come and tell a story.
I'm sure that you are thinking that -
It is a child! - No! It's my darned cat!
Who will not settle on her mat
Until she gets her story.

Irene Beattie

They Don't Hold Grudges

They clubbed his little sisters
then clubbed his brothers too,
his mother then they laid hands on
with my pal the next to do.
He ran and ran and ran
till all his strength was spent.
He knew he could never go back there,
for they just would not relent.
He came to me just plain worn out
within a minute he was asleep,
I cradled him as he slept on
knowing this little chap I'd keep.
Just can't believe his nature,
he sees everyone as friend,
holds no grudges, holds no bitterness
from when he saw his family's end.
I'd like to be like my little cat,
no harm in him to see,
I'd like to be as welcoming
yes, his traits I'd like for me.

Rosie Hues

A Cat's Life

I wake up at four and fancy a drink
No choice for me! I lick from the sink
Now that's OK, for me some days
But not when you haven't
Cleaned the soap away!

It's 7am, I stretch out on the bed
Clean all my paws and scratch my head
Run down the stairs to have some food
But the bowls are empty
So don't mean to be rude.

When I scratch on your door
And screech out instead
Then fight my way in and jump on your bed
Only to be kicked in the head.

So guess it's Sunday
As you still haven't stirred
And mumble something that
Sounds like a swear word.

So I squat on the floor
And leave you a turd
Now come on, be fair
My belly was sore
I can't run down and open the door.

I've still not had breakfast
And its quarter to three
That's when you finally
Decide to feed me.

So now I'm quite happy
And curl up on the couch
And then you decide
To chuck me out.

I sit on the window ledge
Looking within
You're eating roast chicken
Please let me in.

It's getting dark and starting to rain
The tomcat is waiting to jump me again.

They say a cat's life
Is exciting and free
Well, I'd rather be you
Would you want to be me?

Karen Ferrari

Sooky

It started with a farm outcast
With doleful eyes, hesitant paws
Shall I get a life or not, I miaow
They like me! Food, a roof, warm milk.

Now I know they're mine for good
They tell me things like nice day
Going out, you came home Sooky
I hadn't been so far, just sleepy.

And Christmas I get a ball or mouse or toy
I pretend it's like a mouse I know next door
I sometimes snarl and spit and claw
Pretend I'm wild - but they don't mind.

Pam Mills

Bella

Bella's our bunny
We love her so much
She lives in our house
Instead of a hutch
She likes to play tag
And chases our heels
She lies under the table
When we're eating our meals
She likes to keep all her four feet
Safely down on the floor
And when we feed her
She always wants more
Bella's a cutie you have to agree
And is definitely one of the family!

Stella Mortazavi

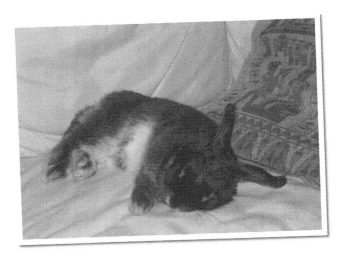

Eric

Lettuce leaves
I love to munch
Cucumber
Is for my lunch
Carrot sticks
For extra crunch
Dill and parsley
In a bunch
Lush green grass
From the local park
Tremble if I hear
Dogs bark
I like corners
Nice and dark
In cardboard boxes
I leave my mark
Scared of vets
Hate the smell
Even though
He says I'm well
Don't trust him
He made me yell
His vaccination
Was just Hell!
My owner
Likes to cuddle me
Snuggle close
For company
Safe and warm
Feeling drowsy
Bedtime for this
Sleepy Cavy!

Debra Webb

Our Sam

Our Sam was so special and if cats could talk
You'd swear he was asking to go for a walk.
He'd leap in the car, when we went for a spin
We'd creep out the back way, but he would jump in.
He'd know when we planned to go out for a trip
And expect to be taken and in he would nip.
To ride on the back of the car window seat
He'd roll on his back, as his joy was complete.
He loved to go out for his walks by the sea
Escorted by Alan, my husband, and me.
The looks we would get were a joy to behold
With Sam on the rocks and appearing so bold.
He'd walk on ahead and sniff under the trees
We'd look for him then; he'd be there by my knees.
But the thing that you'd never believe could be true
Was that when you called Sam, he'd come running to you.
Yes, an out of the ordinary cat you'll agree
He'll always be special to Alan and me.

Tanya Silva

My Little Dog

I would like to tell you, of my little dog,
Who, I must admit, at times is a trog.
He is rather unsociable, and is quite a tyke
And Lord help anyone, who passes on a bike.

Children beware; he will chase you down the street,
He will run at your ankles and try to trip your feet.
He will steal your ball and run away,
You will find it chewed up, the very next day.

He stares at you, with his sparkly black eyes,
He is not naive enough to believe your lies.
He sees right through you, when he gives you that stare,
He will give you a nudge to let you know that he's there.

He behaves so well, when we go in the car
Whether just a short trip, or a drive somewhere far.
He will sit at the window of the passenger seat
Or down in the footwell on somebody's feet.

He chases cats, until they show him their claws,
At this point he runs, and hides in his paws.
He runs at the pigeons that land for some seed
And then he eats what is left of their feed.

It's not very fun when he needs walking in the rain,
When it's wet and gloomy, it can be quite a pain.
But he is very alert as he wanders the park
Watching for danger and shadows in the dark.

He chases his tail; does he know that it's his?
Angry at himself, he gets in a tiz
With his ball in his mouth he barks at the door,
Getting all giddy, he slips across the wooden floor.

Despite all of his faults, he is loyal and true,
He will always be on guard and the first to protect you.
He will warn away who he thinks a threat
And one of these days, you may be in his debt.

182

He is a member of our family, our treasure and joy
And at Christmas, we always get him a new toy.
He will be nine in October and he's set in his ways
But still a spring in his step when he runs and plays.

Hannah Ruston

Naughty Cat

Hey naughty cat
Don't chase that little rat
He is really cute and very sweet
He may look tasty for you to eat
I know you want something to munch
But please don't turn him into your lunch
He nibbled your top and stole your keys
Now all he wants is some cheesy cheese
But you don't know, you have no clue
That I am so much bigger than you
So if you chase that cute little rat
I will chase you, naughty cat.

Marinela Reka

Two Sisters Saved

A dusty country road, southern Italy, late autumn still steamy and hot
A car boot is opened, furtive glances, someone hoping to be out of earshot
As he lifts the cardboard box, squeals break through the air
Tiny helpless creatures yelping cries of fear and despair
Abandoned by the roadside, the man drives off with one thought
What am I supposed to do with ten puppies, keep them I cannot!

Left to be run over or starved to death could have been their terrible fate
But a kind passer-by saved the puppies and a good kennel did locate
In the north, near Milan, they would stand much more of a chance
There they were sent, and put on the Internet where many could glance
So the ten cute half Labrador puppies one by one were adopted
Brothers Andy and Fabio when they saw them were truly besotted.

For Kimba the black one, and Peggy the blonde,
two good homes had been found
On Lake Maggiore two large houses with gardens,
fields and woods all around
The two doggy sisters, Peggy and Kimba,
on a regular basis meet and can play
Living with other saved dogs,
Peggy with Judy, Kimba with Coco and Mandy
Little Alexander, the new baby, has his five furry friends
Entranced by their antics, their affection one contends.

Kimba has a favourite pastime, she likes to catch snakes
None poisonous luckily for the sport in which she partakes
Fearless with a raucous bark to frighten any thief
She growls, guarding the house, for she is the chief
However short a time she hasn't seen you, a present is brought
A large leaf, unpaid bill, magazine or the snake she's just caught.

Thanks for the joy and companionship that these lovely dogs give
Hoping that their brothers and sisters also have a good life to live
Let's spare a thought for all the dogs abandoned and cruelly treated
The animals which out of care, love and affection have been cheated
May the British love of animals spread far and wide
So no more poor dogs are abandoned by the roadside.

Jennifer Rundle

My Pet Cat

I have a cat
A kitten through and through
When I'm having breakfast
He eats his too.

He likes to rub himself around my legs
To show that all is good
And when he begins to purr I know
He's saying more than words ever could

If you find him curled up fast asleep
Just don't disturb him or intrude
It's best to let a sleeping cat lie
Until he decides he wants some food.

He has lots of toys
Scattered all over the floor
But just a few minutes of play
Makes him want to sleep some more.

Sometimes when he's angry
His purr turns to a hiss and a spit
And although he's scratched me more than once
I wouldn't change him not a bit.

Hannah Galloway (10)

For Lucy . . . Despite All You Do

I found paw prints all over my chair today
I'm presuming that they are from you
But as you sit there looking so innocent
I know that this cannot be true

My shoe went missing yesterday
It had wandered under your bed
I know that the chew marks cannot be yours
As you had only just been fed

The water all over the kitchen floor
Must have jumped right out of your bowl
As providing me with cold wet socks
Cannot have been your ultimate goal

I know that the hole in the garden
Must have appeared of its own accord
Even though you are sitting there, covered in mud
Looking like you expect a reward

It's the big soulful eyes that do it
I ignore the destruction I see
As I know that despite all the mess that you make
You're just being the best dog you can be

So I'll keep spending money on chew toys
Even though it's my shoes you prefer
I'll keep on ignoring the paw prints
That cover my favourite chair

I'll fill in the holes in the garden
And mop up the water you throw
As despite all trouble you cause every day
I love you more than you'll ever know.

Wendy Olsen

Winston The Wonder Dog

(Winston passed away 12th October 2007 after a fourteen month fight against Caridomyopathy. He was my companion for nine years. The hurt at his loss still rips at my heart and reduces me to tears. I shall never love another the way I loved him. I love and miss you my dearest Winston.)

You were the world to me
That smiling face secured you a place
In the hearts of our extended family tree
Although now gone
Your legend lives on
Through tales of wonder and glee
So rest in peace my legendary beast
You still mean the world to me.

Deborah Louise Butler-Stevens

I Won't Find You There

The evening's loyal amber stripes
And sweetly spiced warm air
Cutting through the orchard grass
I won't find you there

The darkness falls and smothers all
Brings tears that are quite rare
Swimming in the moonlit pond
I won't find you there

The wind whispers secrets, stories
To anyone who'll care
To perch outside and listen
I won't find you there

But sprawled out by the laughing fire
The crackling flames' lair
My lovely darling pussy cat
I have found you there!

Elizabeth Seal Johnson (13)

Max The Mad Mutt

'Please can we have a dog, Mum? That's all I have ever wanted!'
Pleaded my youngest son again to which I was a little daunted
After some family thought we agreed a spaniel could bring us joy
So off we went to buy a pup, a handsome chocolate brown boy

He was cute with enchanting eyes and long velvet to the touch ears
My son cuddled him tight, a picture of love to eliminate all my fears
How hard could it be to own a dog and welcome him to our family life?
As novices, we soon would see, he was fun but caused some strife

The breeder had called him Mr D'arcy but we chose another name
We decided to call him Max, but so many other dogs are called the same
Trying to teach Max recall whilst out strolling in the park
Only invited other hounds to wander over and bark

So off to puppy classes to learn commands and how to behave
But only chaos did ensue, it was more a spaniel rave
Our Max failed to learn anything at all but his friendly little ways
Give us much delight, his motto is surely 'happy days'

He likes his walks where he can roam the heath or along the beach
It's even better if there's a sandwich well within his reach
He stole some bread from a bathing couple and took off with great speed
The angry pair screamed aloud and demanded he was put back on a lead

Obedience is not his thing; in fact he enjoys digging or a chew
Mostly it's our shoes or socks but a bra will often do
He's a scamp, a chancer but he only really wants to play
His loving welcoming nature is the joy he brings our way

We've come to love our rascal mutt and all the funny things he does
Chasing birds, dirty paws, slobbery licks and pooping in the shrubs
In just a year young Max has become our cherished family treasure
A dog will love you always; it's a love you cannot measure.

Maggie Day

Call Of The Tiger

Always dashing around the garden
Flying up tree trunks after the birds
Miaowing to stop inclement weather
She's a smart cat of very few words
Forever alert to steal your chair
And nibble on a dangling wire
Happily offering her tummy for strokes
Before toasting in front of the fire
Playing hide-and-seek in the boxes
Then chewing any book edge or pen
She enjoys playing pounce on the blanket
And then inside forms a cosy den.

Lovingly she brushes against your leg
And every day she warms your lap
Following along to bed each night
Where she snuggles to take a nap
Twitching and grabbing with her paws
And throwing her tail askew
I wonder what happens in her dreams
She might be chasing a mouse or a shrew.

Regular patches and long black stripes
Adorn her fine soft glossy coat
Well-defined necklaces in her fur
Add a proper and respectable note
Yet she leaps up with unbridled excitement
When you push the lounge door ajar
And looks straight up into your eyes
A loving stare that says you're a star.

Richard Savory

Pet A Phasmida

We're members of the arthropods
Phasmida to be precise
It comes from the Greek word, Phasma
Meaning ghostly unusual sight!

Stick insects or walking sticks
Are how we're better known
With twig-like bodies, long and thin
By six months we're full-grown.

We can blend into the background
Camouflage ourselves and hide
Away from predators that stalk us
Including birds, bats and mice.

We come from tropic regions and
Here's a clever fact
If we lose one of our precious legs
We can grow another back.

We hang motionless by daylight
Little suckers on our feet
If disturbed unnecessarily
We play dead, our enemies to beat.

We do not prey on others
As we're veggie through and through
But gorge ourselves on hawthorn leaves
Brambles, roses, privet too!

Moulting is the way we grow
Our skins we shed and eat
This helps preserve our proteins
Scientifically it's a feat!

We like to live with other sticks
We need companions too
We're easy to look after and
Would love a home with you.

Next time your child is lonely
And wants to get a pet
Give a phasmida a thought then
We very seldom need the vet!

Sarah Hickson

Ode To The Four-Legged Friend

Faithful, friendly and full of fun
A dog is Man's best friend
Loving, caring and funny
Best friend till the end
They love having attention
Playing fetch and doing tricks
They love you when you buy a bone
Even more when you throw a stick
I love my four-legged friend
On him I can depend
What are those words they say?
'A dog is Man's best friend.'

Donna Salisbury

The Siamogg

A long, pointy face, a kinked tail,
A strong personality,
He'll be there for me, without fail -
Quantity and quality.

A Siamese by nature, and
He's stripy, with yellow too,
A white bib, two white feet - so grand -
Other colours, there, to view.

The Siamese low voice is there,
He talks a hell of a lot.
His screaming will give you a scare,
The enemies can just rot.

Tygae Tigerus is his name,
I call him my Siamogg.
He likes cuddles - and to play the game -
Chasing mice and the odd frog.

He's twelve years old and is heavy
To carry around in my arms.
Solid, big-boned and is ready
To show off all of his charms.

Roslyn Fielding

Home

There they stood, battered and worn
Bony and shaking. Rejected, forlorn
Not the pooches of kings.
No proud heads held high
Infections, bald patches
But a twinkle in their eye.

When I looked closer, they smiled, eyes wide
Somehow I knew they were eyes that had cried.
Not a mummy to love them
No owner to care
There was no way on this Earth
I was leaving them there.

Home they came to start a new life with me
Though I had to insist they said goodbye to the fleas.
Not an aching tooth
No fleas jumping to bite
Someone could have told me
They'd bark through night!

My husband looked in horror as one ran away
When we went to collect them the very next day.
Not very appreciative
No 'thank you kind sir'
But we took them and nurtured them
And now they even have fur!

'We could have a pedigree Lab,' he'd said, 'chocolate in colour,'
I shook my head, for I'd have no other.
Not a Doberman nor Corgi
'No, I won't take any buts . . .
They called to me,' I told him
'OK,' he said, 'we'll take the flea-ridden mutts!'

They needed a home, like so many others
Since then, I've even given them two brothers!
Not the four-legged kind
No patter of puppy feet
But more gentle babysitters
You will never ever met.

She still wees on the floor at sudden sounds
He moults enough hair to fill an eiderdown but
Not a tear to be seen and
They smile every day
Ever since I took them away.

Four years on, and
They're cute as buttons.
Their past still haunts them
And they eat like glutens.

So next time you visit the pound for a puppy
Don't pass the ones who look lumpy, not fluffy.
All they need is a family of their own
Where they can hold their heads high
And know they are home.

Tara Deakin

The Menacing Cat We Can't Live Without

My cat is called Guinness
He'll bite, scratch and hiss

He has evil eyes ever glued on the prize
Look at this smug cat in his cunning disguise

If you think the sofa's yours think again - he'll be waiting
Now you're the prey Guinness is so sure to be baiting

What a sight my dad and Guinness are when side by side
As they watch for one another, pounce, cackle and hide.

His eyes glow threateningly when he is bad
Watching out for my thunderous stomping dad

Guinness hides in dark corners waiting and grim
An ambush from shadows when lights are still dim

Laugh at the tricks that Guinness plays on him
Fighting off this angry cat with life and limb

It's not a pretty sight when he has to be pilled
The furniture replaced and the vases refilled

To be on the safe side, don't dress him in pink
He's harmless really - he won't hurt you (I think)

As my cat, how many a foe he has silenced
With his menacing glare - one you must licence

The cats in the street nickname Guinness the 'feline Bond'
Stirred but not shaken, he mews at the bar by the pond

His black dining coat, white shirt and dickie, very posh
One milk martini, now, let's play, hand over the dosh

Whatever you do, please do not touch his tummy
So many bandages you'll look like a mummy

My cat is not evil, just misunderstood
He doesn't prowl in boots, cape and a black hood (much)

Guinness loves me though - for that I am grateful
Without our Guinness, life would be hateful

If I were you I wouldn't dress him in pink
He's harmless really - you might survive (I think).

Elizabeth Hughes

198

My Cat Katie

My cat is called Katie
She is black and white
She fell down the toilet
And went out of sight.

We called up the plumber
But there was nothing she could do
When Katie came back up again
She was covered in poo!

She was outside one Christmas
Came back covered in snow,
Her belly was bigger
Boy, didn't I know.

From one look of her eye
And the twitch of her nose
What she'd been up to
As she struck up a pose.

One night sat by the fire
I heard a loud miaow
Coming from upstairs
Oh no, please not now.

With my parents out
I didn't know what to do
I ran up the stairs
And then into the loo

Where Katie was waiting
For me to see
The three little kittens
That were so cute and lovely.

My cat is called Katie
And she has three kittens
There's Spot and there's Ginger
But the cutest of all is called Mittens.

Roseanne Lapidge
Lipson Community College, Plymouth

It's Too Hot For Me

I've just one thing to say
To you humans in May
It's far, far too hot for me
Why can't you just see?

I want to sit in my house
While I catch a juicy mouse
I want to lounge on the rug
While I drink from my mug.

I've just one thing to say
To you humans in May
It's far, far too hot for me
Why can't you just see?

You need to look after me
All I want is a cup of tea
Without it I might flee
Why can't you just see?

Naomi Gibson
Lipson Community College, Plymouth

Morphi

I look out into the darkness that is the night
Following the cries of a cat out of sight.
The sun, the moon, the winter breeze,
The eyes that glow like moon in seas.
Your padded feet, your silver whiskers
Dancing to the sound of your whimpers.
Your limp, your grace, your fluffy face,
The way you sit, the way you chase.
The way you sit at the dinner table
Even if the chair is not stable.
I love to see you and stroke you
To watch the silly things you do,
Love the way you nibble on my toes
Your fur is as soft as a velvet rose.
I love the way you sit in the basket
And get fur on Mum's favourite blanket.
I love your golden sunbeam eyes
That search the world, the highest skies.
You sit on my shoulder; you think you're a parrot
And your fur's as orange as a giant carrot.

Hannah Gibson
Lipson Community College, Plymouth

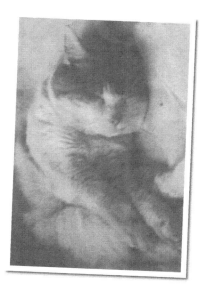

Forward Press Information

We hope you have enjoyed reading this book - and that you will continue to enjoy it in the coming years.

If you like reading and writing poetry drop us a line, or give us a call, and we'll send you a free information pack.

Alternatively if you would like to order further copies of this book or any of our other titles, then please give us a call or log onto our website at www.forwardpress.co.uk

Forward Press Information
Remus House
Coltsfoot Drive
Peterborough
PE2 9JX
(01733) 890099